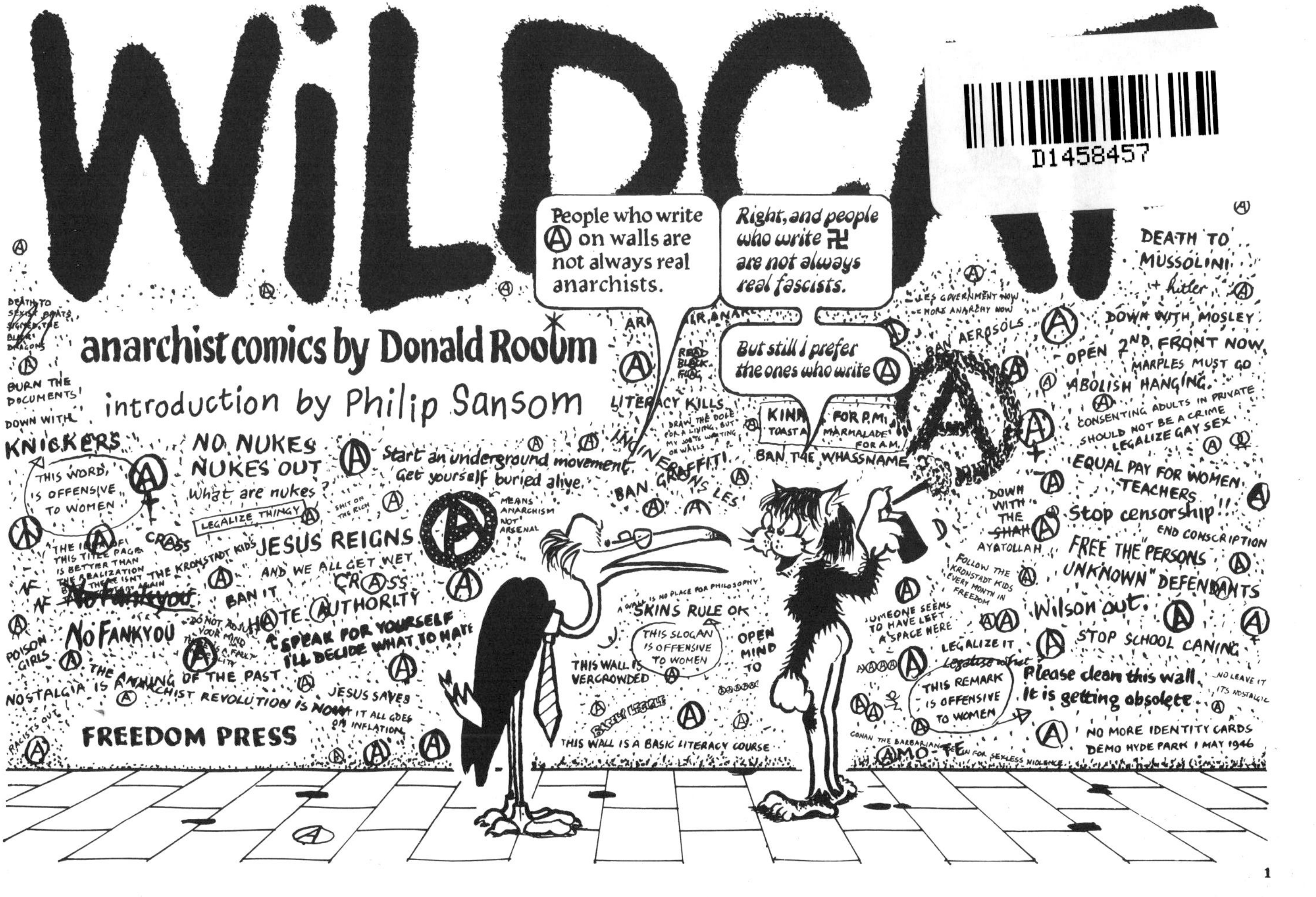
WILDCAT
anarchist comics by Donald Rooum
introduction by Philip Sansom
FREEDOM PRESS
People who write Ⓐ on walls are not always real anarchists.
Right, and people who write 卐 are not always real fascists.
But still I prefer the ones who write Ⓐ
DEATH TO MUSSOLINI + hitler
DOWN WITH MOSLEY
OPEN 2ND FRONT NOW
MARPLES MUST GO
ABOLISH HANGING
CONSENTING ADULTS IN PRIVATE SHOULD NOT BE A CRIME
LEGALIZE GAY SEX
EQUAL PAY FOR WOMEN TEACHERS
Stop censorship!!
END CONSCRIPTION
FREE THE "PERSONS UNKNOWN" DEFENDANTS
Wilson out.
STOP SCHOOL CANING
Please clean this wall. It is getting obsolete
NO LEAVE IT ITS NOSTALGIC
NO MORE IDENTITY CARDS
DEMO HYDE PARK 1 MAY 1946
THIS REMARK IS OFFENSIVE TO WOMEN
LEGALIZE IT
SOMEONE SEEMS TO HAVE LEFT A SPACE HERE
FOLLOW THE KRONSTADT KIDS EVERY MONTH IN FREEDOM
DOWN WITH THE SHAH
AYATOLLAH
BAN AEROSOLS
LITERACY KILLS
BAN THE WHASSNAME
SKINS RULE OK
THIS SLOGAN IS OFFENSIVE TO WOMEN
OPEN MIND TO
THIS WALL IS A BASIC LITERACY COURSE
BURN THE DOCUMENTS!
DOWN WITH KNICKERS
THIS WORD IS OFFENSIVE TO WOMEN
NO NUKES
NUKES OUT
What are nukes?
LEGALIZE THINGY
Start an underground movement. Get yourself buried alive.
JESUS REIGNS
AND WE ALL GET WET
CRASS
BAN IT
HATE AUTHORITY
SPEAK FOR YOURSELF I'LL DECIDE WHAT TO HATE
NO FANKYOU
POISON GIRLS
NOSTALGIA IS ANARCHIST REVOLUTION IS NOW
JESUS SAVES
IT ALL GOES ON INFLATION
MEANS ANARCHISM NOT ARSENAL
THE KRONSTADT KIDS

Published by Freedom Press
in Angel Alley
84b Whitechapel High Street
London E1 7QX.

ISBN 0 900384 30 1

Printed in Great Britain by
Aldgate Press, London.

CATALOGUING GUIDE

Rooum, Donald
Sansom, Philip
Wildcat anarchist comics

Anarchism 321.07
Cartoons 741.9055 ROO

First published November 1985
Reprinted August 1987
Reprinted March 1995
Reprinted December 2004

Incinerons les documents!!
Burn the documents!!
Are you with the insurgents of Lyons?
No. I'm with the C.I.A.
Shred the Klaus Barbie file!!
Rooum

Introduction

Donald Rooum and I first met in the late summer of 1944 and I would be a liar if I said I remembered the occasion. He was at that time a not-so-callow 16-year-old who had come south from his native Bradford to spend a working holiday in the Kentish hop-fields.

On his first Sunday off work he came to London to have a look at the famous 'Speaker's Corner' at Marble Arch - the North-east corner of Hyde Park. Here it was that Donald heard his first pearls of wisdom falling from the lips of anarchist speakers. At the park gates he also found me, selling anarchist literature, and bought a copy of the anarchist journal of that time - *War Commentary* - and a copy of Alexander Berkman's *ABC of Anarchism*.

On his return to Bradford once all the hops were in, he sent a subscription to *War Commentary* and set about making contacts with other anarchists in Lancashire and Yorkshire. Within a year the war came to an end and Britain was rejoicing in a Labour government - which decided to retain military conscription, calling up all healthy young men for two years from the age of 18. Donald was 18 in April 1946 and registered as a conscientious objector, but, yielding to family pressure, allowed himself to be sucked into the army in January 1947. His two mis-spent years had one useful result: an army resettlement grant helped to finance him for four years on a design course at Bradford School of Art.

Over the 1949 August Bank Holiday weekend, Donald attended the annual Anarchist Summer School, held that year in Liverpool, and made a memorable impact on the anarchist movement in general. Among the speakers were Tony Gibson, Albert Meltzer, and another whose name I forbear to mention, whose lecture was reported in *Freedom* in the kindly words: 'The importance ... attached to the influence of superstition on modern customs and recreations aroused a good deal of controversy among the audience'. I well remember Comrade Rooum's contribution to that controversy, when he stood up and said, in his thick Bradford accent: 'It's all baloney!'

Pricking the balloons of baloney is, of course, the cartoonist's art, and when I found later that Donald was developing that art, I jumped at the possibility of using him. It gives me great pleasure, as they say, to state that I gave him his first opportunity to appear regularly in print.

By 1952, having had six years as industrial editor on *Freedom* and a reasonably successful pamphlet with the highly unoriginal title *Syndicalism the Workers' Next Step*, I felt ready to start a specifically anarcho-syndicalist paper, not in any way as a rival to, but in tandem with, *Freedom*. In company with three other comrades, I launched *The Syndicalist* in May 1952.

Being responsible not only for the practical editing but also for production and design, I decided we needed a comic strip. I wrote to Donald Rooum and promptly got a reply, including a couple of sample strips, centred around a character called 'Scissor Bill'. Evidently Donald had been reading the literature of the Industrial Workers of the World, or 'Wobblies', who had created the nick-name Scissor Bill for a really stupid lackey of the boss.

To be honest, the Scissor Bill drawings were pretty crude. But they were, after all, about a character whose understanding of capitalism was pretty crude too, who would think nothing of working for nine hours on a production line making cars - and then going home on a bike. The strip was a popular feature of *The Syndicalist*, which unhappily folded after a year.

In January 1954 Donald came to London. He had trained himself as an outdoor speaker on a platform in Market Street, Bradford, and quickly proved an asset on the London Anarchist Group platform in Hyde Park, where we had a large group of speakers and a regular audience. He had a strong voice and his deadly logic reduced many a heckler to frustrated silence.

In the spring of 1954 we tired of using temporary rooms over pubs for our indoor meetings, and decided to find suitable premises and establish our own meeting place and social club. Donald was one of the Founder Members - an honour that brought more sweat than 'apence. He reminds me that he worked till 4am on May 1st 1954, covering the dust of the concrete floor with red paint, to be ready for opening night.

The Malatesta Club (so called because Malatesta was the one historical anarchist we could all agree upon as totally OK) was opened every night for the next four years by teams of voluntary workers,

WILDCAT
War is an outlet for individual aggression.
Eh?
Rub, bish! Modern war is a matter of patient calculation and exact button pushing.
Individual aggression is more like this.
THUMP!
Rooum

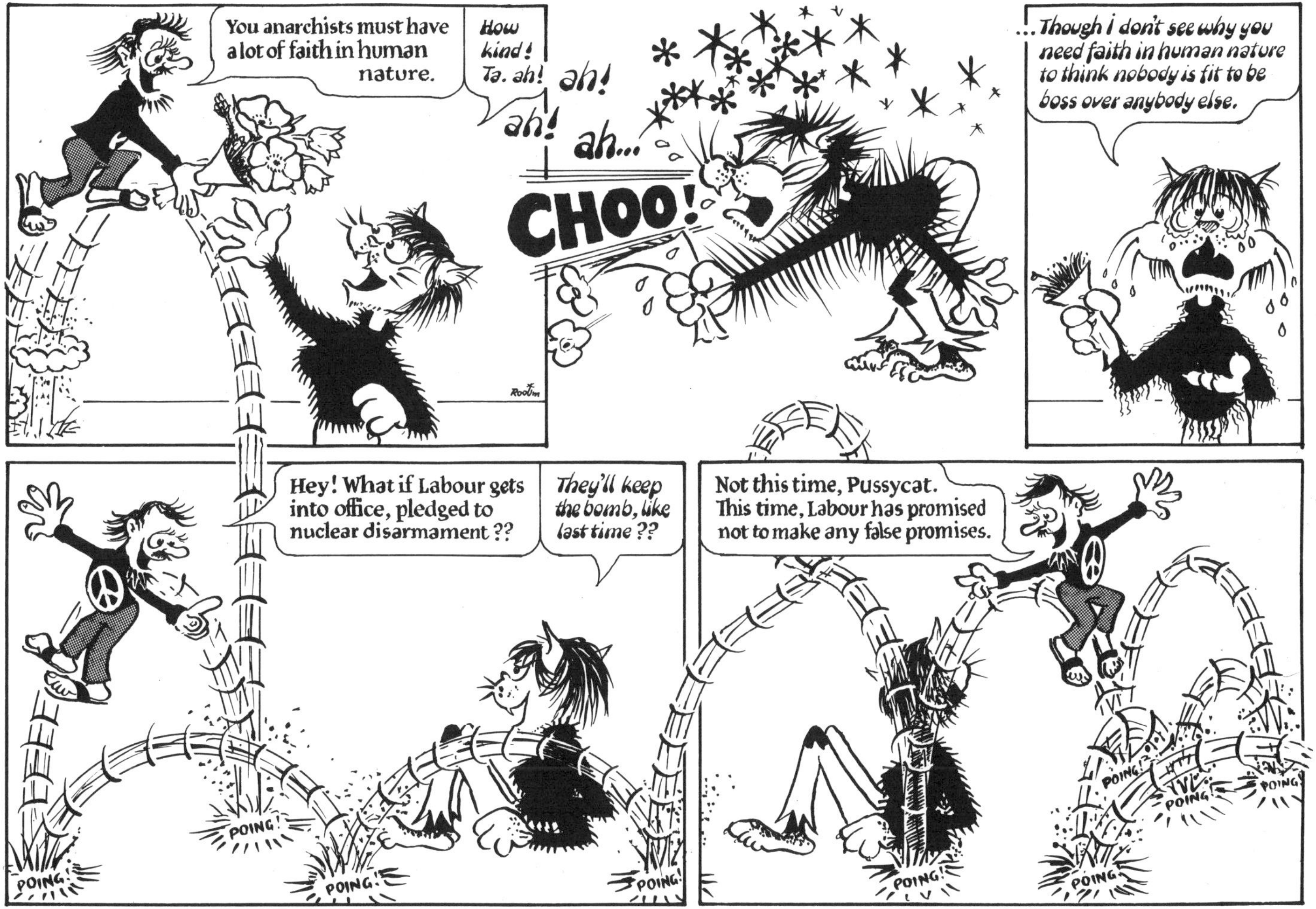
You anarchists must have a lot of faith in human nature.
How kind! Ta. ah!
ah! ah! ah...
CHOO!
...Though I don't see why you need faith in human nature to think nobody is fit to be boss over anybody else.
Hey! What if Labour gets into office, pledged to nuclear disarmament??
They'll keep the bomb, like last time??
POING!
POING!
POING!
POING!
Not this time, Pussycat. This time, Labour has promised not to make any false promises.
POING!
POING!
POING!
POING!
POING!
POING!

including Donald and his companion Irene Brown. Activities included lectures, discussion meetings, making the place available for other groups (including an African group whose members later became cabinet ministers, and the famous orator Bonar Thompson), while every Saturday was social and entertainment night. Donald never failed to bring the house down with his rendition of 'Jabberwocky'.

In 1960, single cartoons by Rooum were beginning to appear in journals as diverse as *She, Daily Mirror, Private Eye* and *The Spectator*. From 1962 through to 1971 his political cartoons appeared regularly in *Peace News*, and have attracted enough attention for the originals to have been deposited in the Centre for the Study of Cartoon and Caricature at the University of Kent in Canterbury.

In 1963 however, and however accidentally, Donald Rooum found himself involved in events which have earned him a niche in social and judicial history.

July 1963, and London was honoured by a State Visit by King Paul and Queen Frederica of the Hellenes - the king and queen of a Greece at that time suffering under a vicious right-wing regime which still held prisoners taken during the civil war which followed World War Two. The visit was not well timed, coming as it did soon after the murder by Greek fascists - with police connivance - of Gregory Lambrakis, a left-wing member of the Greek Parliament, who had marched from Marathon to Athens with a number of anti-nuclear demonstrators. Queen Fred, as she became known, had been a member of the Hitler Youth. Our own Queen Elizabeth II and her husband Prince Philip (of Greek extraction) welcomed their royal cousins with open arms.

This was the background for a series of demonstrations by sections of British taxpayers, annoyed, for various reasons,

WILDCAT
Hey!! You're standing on my back !!
Right, Pussycat. We're standing on everybody's back.
Why ??
So that America may stand tall.
HOORAY!
HOORAY!
YIPPEE!
HOORAY!
GROAN !!!
OUCH !!!
Rooum

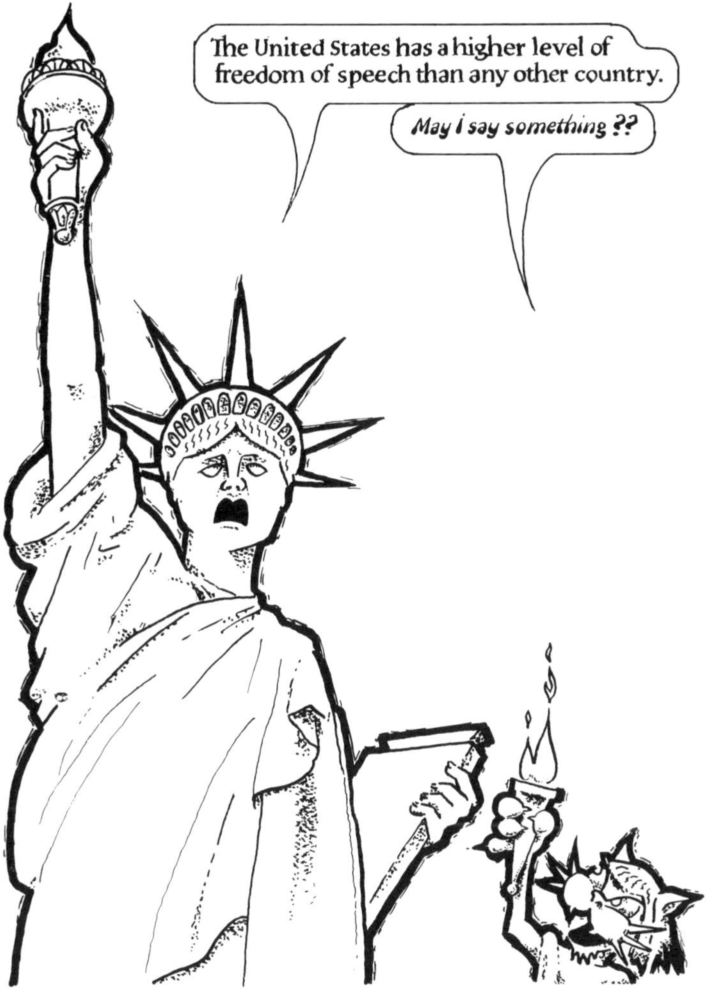
The United States has a higher level of freedom of speech than any other country.
May i say something ??

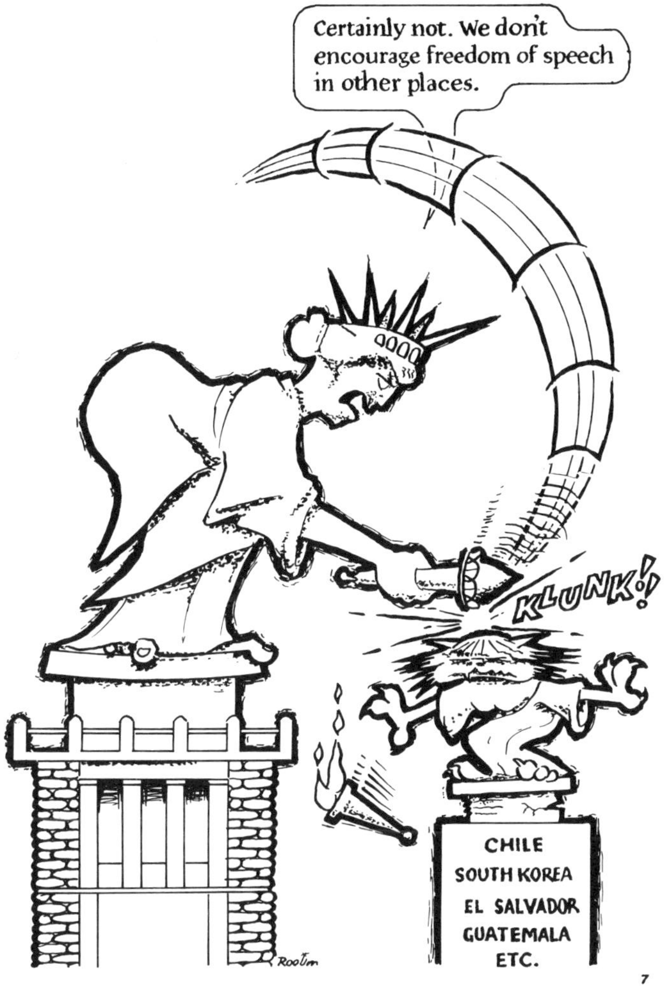
Certainly not. We don't encourage freedom of speech in other places.
KLUNK!
CHILE
SOUTH KOREA
EL SALVADOR
GUATEMALA
ETC.

at having to pick up the tab for this royal shindig. They included persons concerned about the perversion of democracy in Greece (birthplace of democracy), pacifists, nuclear disarmers, communists, militant Christians, Greek and Cypriot left-wingers, and of course anarchists - a wide range of people who don't like reactionary fascists.

On the 11th July 'our' queen was due to arrive at Claridges to have a nosh-up with Queen Fred. About three thousand demonstrators turned up, to find about five thousand police preventing anyone entering a wide arc around Claridges. Donald was among the would-be demonstrators, carrying a modest little banner with the words 'Lambrakis RIP', in the hope of flashing it as the Queen arrived at the hotel. Having failed to penetrate the police cordon, he was walking away from the scene when he was seized by a plain-clothes policeman, told 'You're fuckin' nicked, my old beauty', bundled into a van, taken to a police station, kicked upstairs to a cell and there beaten about the head.

All fairly routine stuff, you might think, but what happened next was less common. The policeman took a bundle from his pocket, unwrapped it to reveal a large piece of brick, and said 'There you are my old darling. Carrying an offensive weapon, you can get two years for that.' Donald refused to sign the list of his property which included the brick.

The policeman who treated Donald so illegally was Detective Sergeant Harold Challenor, a man with a heroic army record and a fine police record of enthusiastic arrests leading to successful convictions - many of them, it later transpired, based upon perjured evidence against individuals plucked off the streets, sometimes (as in this case) purely by chance.

You have only to spend a morning in any magistrates court to see how easily

That Korean passenger plane was spying for the C.I.A. Dead stupid, too. No hope of discovering anything the C.I.A. did not already know.
Then why did you shoot it down??
Because it was there.
Rootm

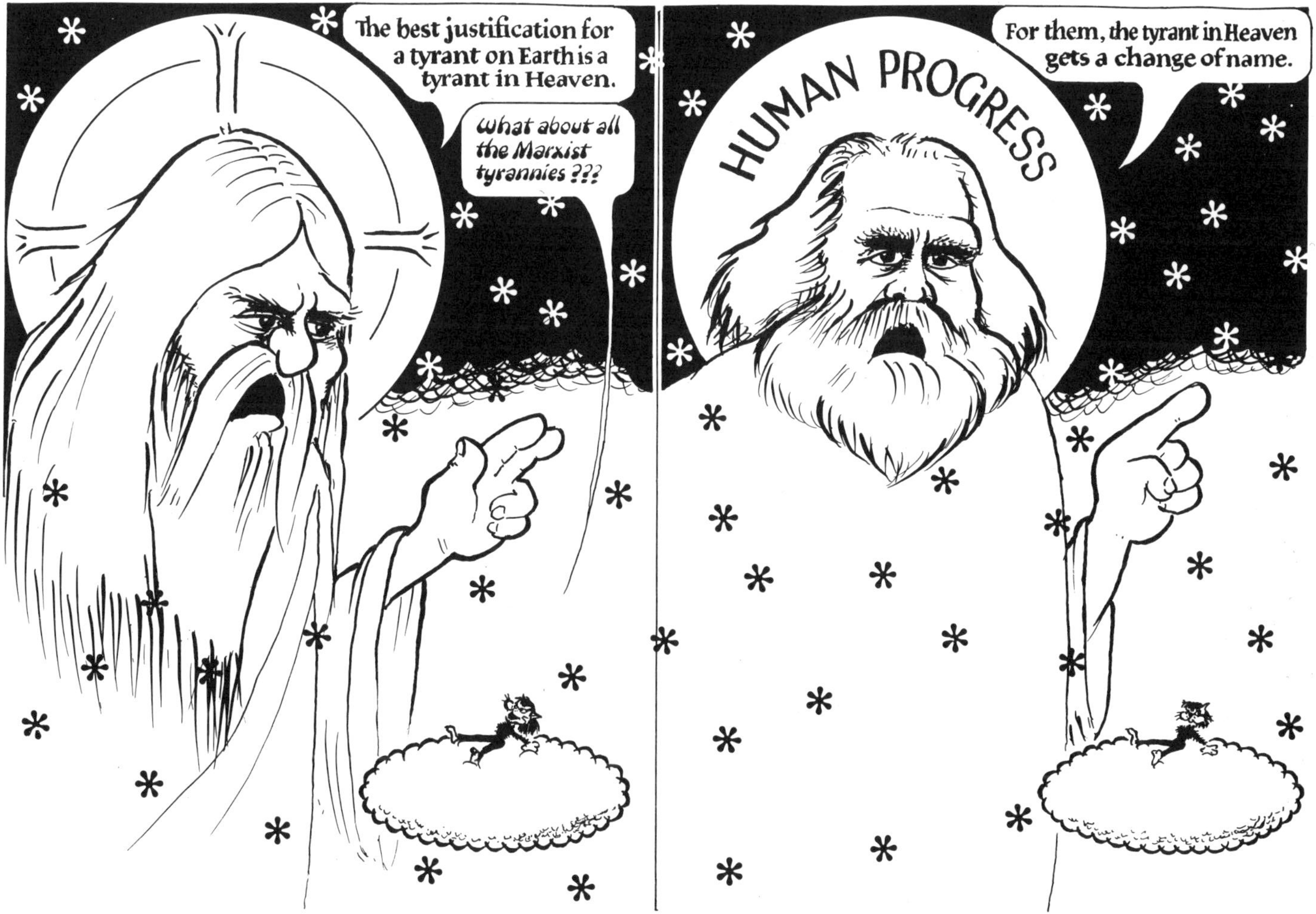
The best justification for a tyrant on Earth is a tyrant in Heaven.
What about all the Marxist tyrannies ???
HUMAN PROGRESS
For them, the tyrant in Heaven gets a change of name.

police evidence goes through on the majority of poor, illiterate, ineffective and inarticulate individuals. But it was D-S Challenor who turned out to be the unfortunate one this time. How was he to know that this time, the one he bundled off to West End Central police station in his usual brutal manner was a 'Stirnerite' anarchist - an individual who put faith in his own strength and intelligence and would fight back against those who misused him? Donald had many friends and comrades who would rally round, knew how to make contact with the National Council for Civil Liberties, and could spot immediately how to refute the 'evidence' of the brick in his pocket.

By the rules, Donald should have been released on bail, but he was kept in custody overnight so there was no doubt that the jacket in which he was arrested was the same jacket in which he appeared before the magistrate the following morning. When he had pleaded 'not guilty' and had the case adjourned, with the help of legal representatives from the NCCL his jacket was whipped away straight from the magistrate's court to a forensic laboratory. An independent expert analyst testified in court that there was not the slightest evidence any of Donald's pockets had ever carried a brick. He even brought test-tubes with samples of unadulterated pocket fluff with no sign of brick dust. Case dismissed.

The ramifications are well documented elsewhere. Briefly, some 26 other cases were re-opened, and Challenor's known victims - some genuine villains convicted on fraudulent evidence, some completely innocent - were pardoned or paid damages or both. Three young constables were imprisoned, senior officers who had connived at Challenor's tactics continued their careers, and Challenor himself was found to be insane and put out to grass. Another example of a rotten apple in a

I'm fighting Nazis. Are you in favour of Nazis?
Of course not, but the Pussycat isn't a Nazi.
Don't give me this hairsplitting nonsense about a distinction between Nazis and other gentiles.
BANGG!!
Rooum

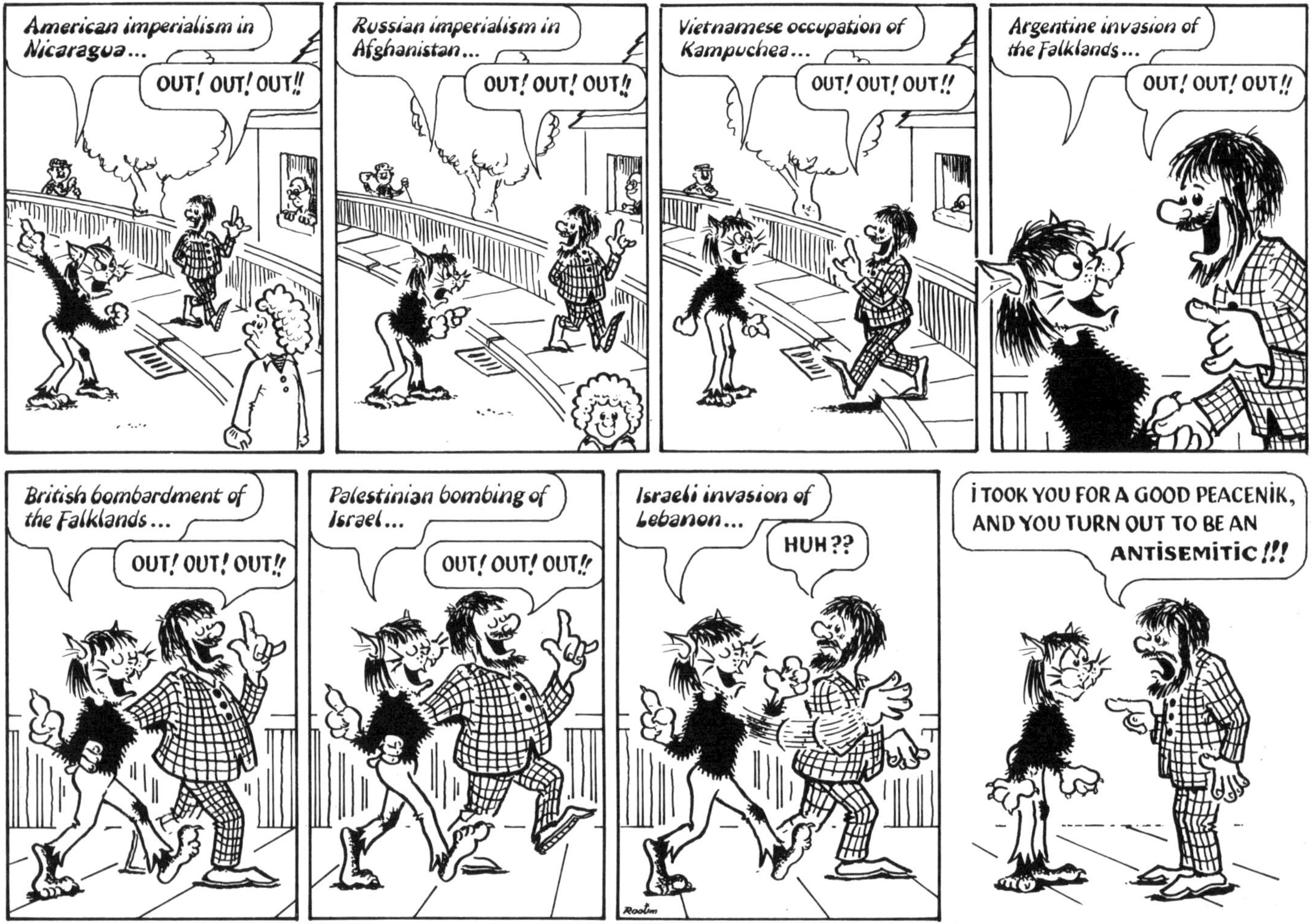
American imperialism in Nicaragua...
OUT! OUT! OUT!!
Russian imperialism in Afghanistan...
OUT! OUT! OUT!!
Vietnamese occupation of Kampuchea...
OUT! OUT! OUT!!
Argentine invasion of the Falklands...
OUT! OUT! OUT!!
British bombardment of the Falklands...
OUT! OUT! OUT!!
Palestinian bombing of Israel...
OUT! OUT! OUT!!
Israeli invasion of Lebanon...
HUH??
Rootim
I TOOK YOU FOR A GOOD PEACENIK, AND YOU TURN OUT TO BE AN ANTISEMITIC!!!

rotten barrel.

Things returned to normal. Ordinary policemen returned to their ordinarily accepted levels of lying, and Donald returned to his peaceful occupation of undermining hypocrisy on his drawing board. By this time he was a master of his craft, full of ideas and with an individual and distinctive style. Here is this volume to prove it.

I was to call on his services on two more occasions. In 1974 I became involved with Wynford Hicks and others in the editing and production of a journal called *Wildcat.* It was an intelligent, investigative, near-anarchist paper, and after an initial disappointment with a cartoonist not of my choosing, we decided to call in Donald Rooum and ask him to create a character called - what else? - 'Wildcat'.

This was a younger, rather gentler pussy than the one we know now, but she developed not only as a strip character, but as a public relations officer and cheer-leader as well. She got angrier as the monthly issues passed and was quite angry when the paper closed in mid-1975.

But she was, as they say in the theatre, only 'resting'. In 1980, a year after I had returned once again to my first love, *Freedom*, I sent out another call for help to Donald (who must have said to himself something like 'Here we go again!'), and the *Freedom* Collective were agreed that the irrascible puss should come down off the tiles and get among the pigeons. She's been causing a flutter ever since, and has been popping up in papers in Germany (speaking impeccable German) and elsewhere. She is a determined, if sometimes perplexed, anarchist cat, fighting always for a sane, logical and basically honest understanding of what a libertarian philosophy of life demands.

Just like Donald Rooum himself, really.

Philip Sansom

This is for your protection.
TICK TICK! TICK! TICK!
N MISSILE
Rub,bish !! it's impossible to obtain protection by threatening suicide with something dangerouser than what you aaaaaaargh !!!
BAM!
Take that, for refusing to be protected.
TICK! TICK! TICK! TICK! TICK!
Rooum

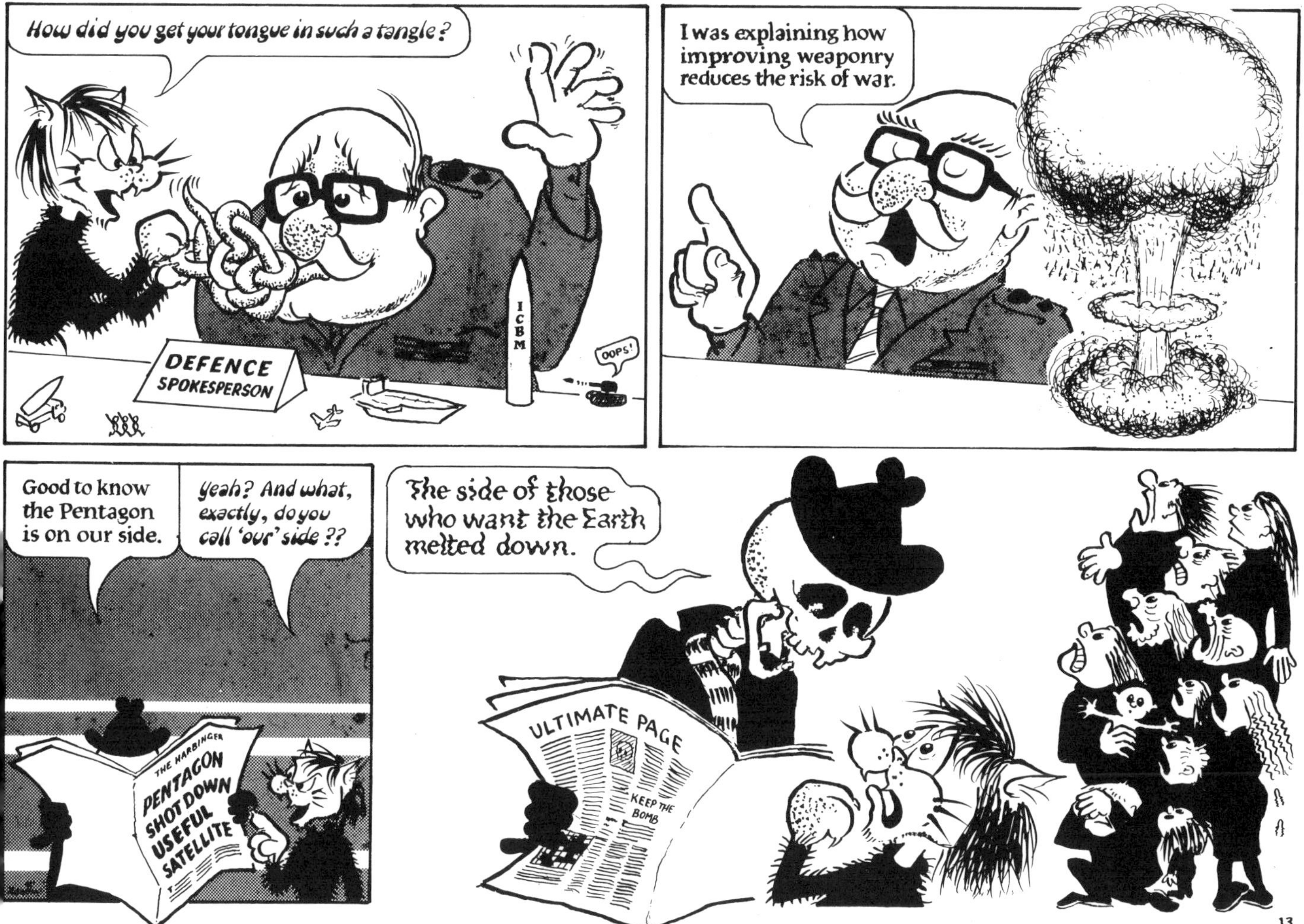
How did you get your tongue in such a tangle?
DEFENCE SPOKESPERSON
ICBM
OOPS!
I was explaining how improving weaponry reduces the risk of war.
Good to know the Pentagon is on our side.
Yeah? And what, exactly, do you call 'our' side??
THE HARBINGER
PENTAGON SHOT DOWN USEFUL SATELLITE
The side of those who want the Earth melted down.
ULTIMATE PAGE
KEEP THE BOMB

A FEW OF THE CHARACTERS WHO APPEAR IN THE "WILDCAT" STRIP

A TYPE OF ANARCHIST

THE FREE-RANGE EGGHEAD

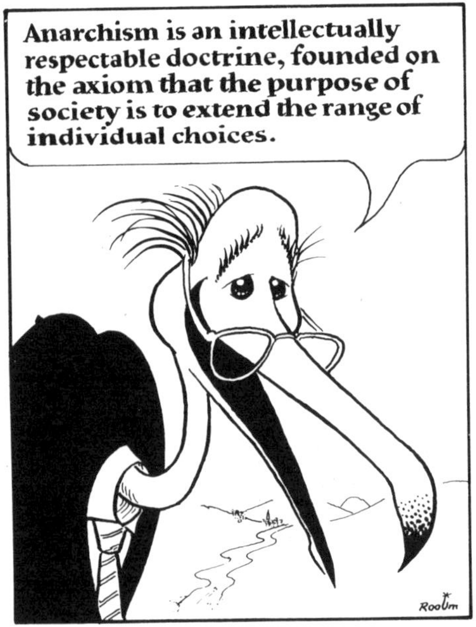
Anarchism is an intellectually respectable doctrine, founded on the axiom that the purpose of society is to extend the range of individual choices.

ANOTHER TYPE OF ANARCHIST

THE REVOLTING PUSSYCAT

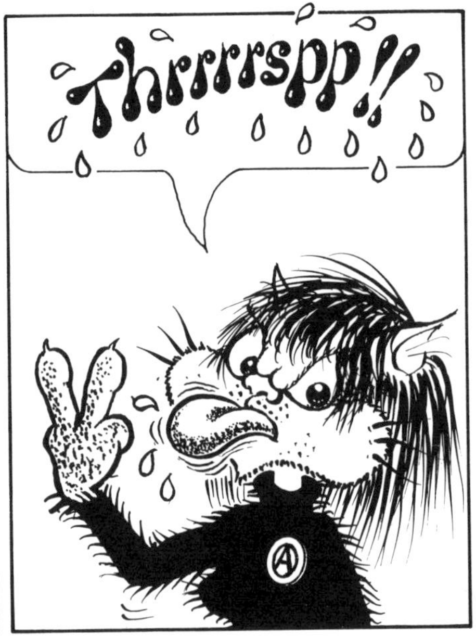
Thrrrrspp!!

A FICTITIOUS TYPE

KARL YUNDT

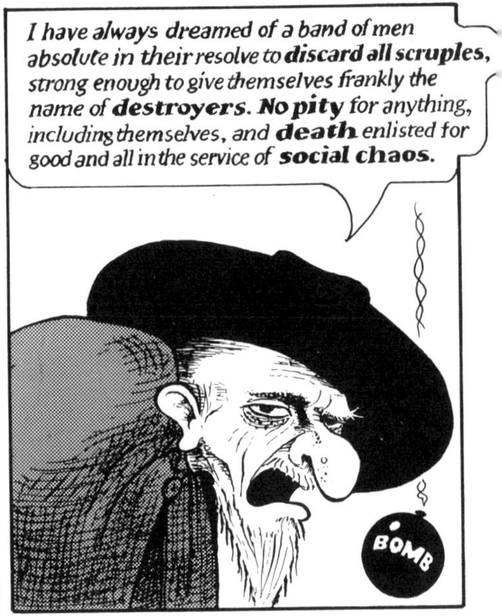
I have always dreamed of a band of men absolute in their resolve to **discard all scruples**, strong enough to give themselves frankly the name of **destroyers**. **No pity** for anything, including themselves, and **death** enlisted for good and all in the service of **social chaos**.
BOMB

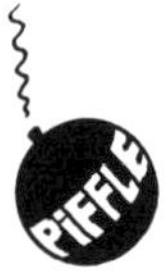
PIFFLE

NOTE. The Egghead appears in a supporting role, because a cartoon is no place for intellectual respectability.

ADDITIONAL NOTE. Karl Yundt does not appear atall, because his attitude is not remotely connected with anarchism, despite his influence on ideas of "anarchism" among the ill-informed. (He began as a character in *The Secret Agent* by Joseph Conrad.)

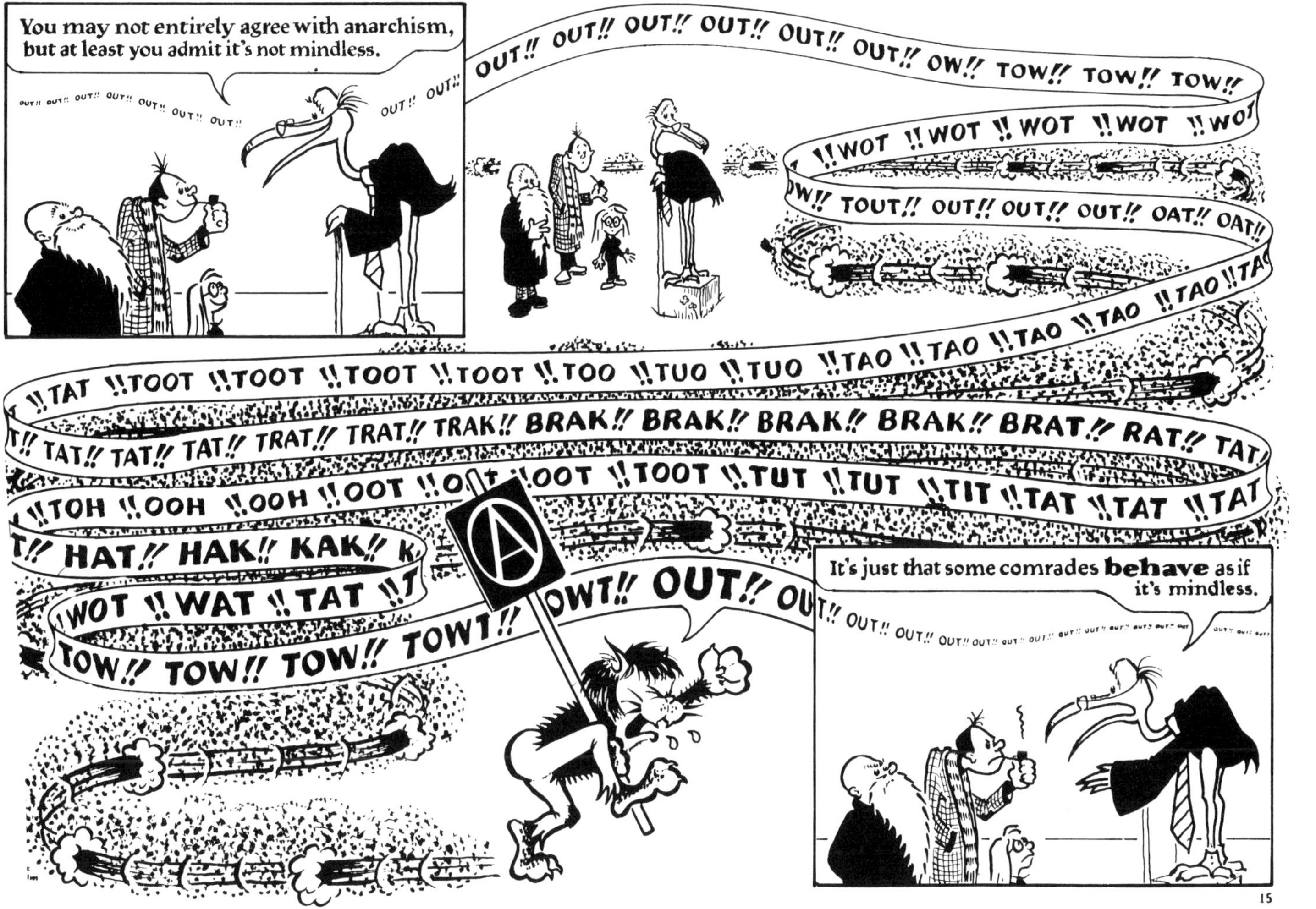

You may not entirely agree with anarchism, but at least you admit it's not mindless.
OUT!! OUT!! OUT!! OUT!! OUT!! OUT!! OUT!! OW!! TOW!! TOW!! TOW!!
!!WOT !!WOT !!WOT !!WOT !!WOT
TOUT!! OUT!! OUT!! OUT!! OAT!! OAT!!
!!TAT !!TOOT !!TOOT !!TOOT !!TOOT !!TOO !!TUO !!TUO !!TAO !!TAO !!TAO !!TAO !!TAO !!TAO
TAT!! TAT!! TAT!! TRAT!! TRAT!! TRAK!! BRAK!! BRAK!! BRAK!! BRAK!! BRAT!! RAT!! TAT
!!TOH !!OOH !!OOH !!OOT !!OOT !!TOOT !!TUT !!TUT !!TIT !!TAT !!TAT !!TAT
HAT!! HAK!! KAK!!
WOT !!WAT !!TAT
TOW!! TOW!! TOW!! TOWT!! OWT!! OUT!! OUT!! OUT!! OUT!!
It's just that some comrades **behave** as if it's mindless.

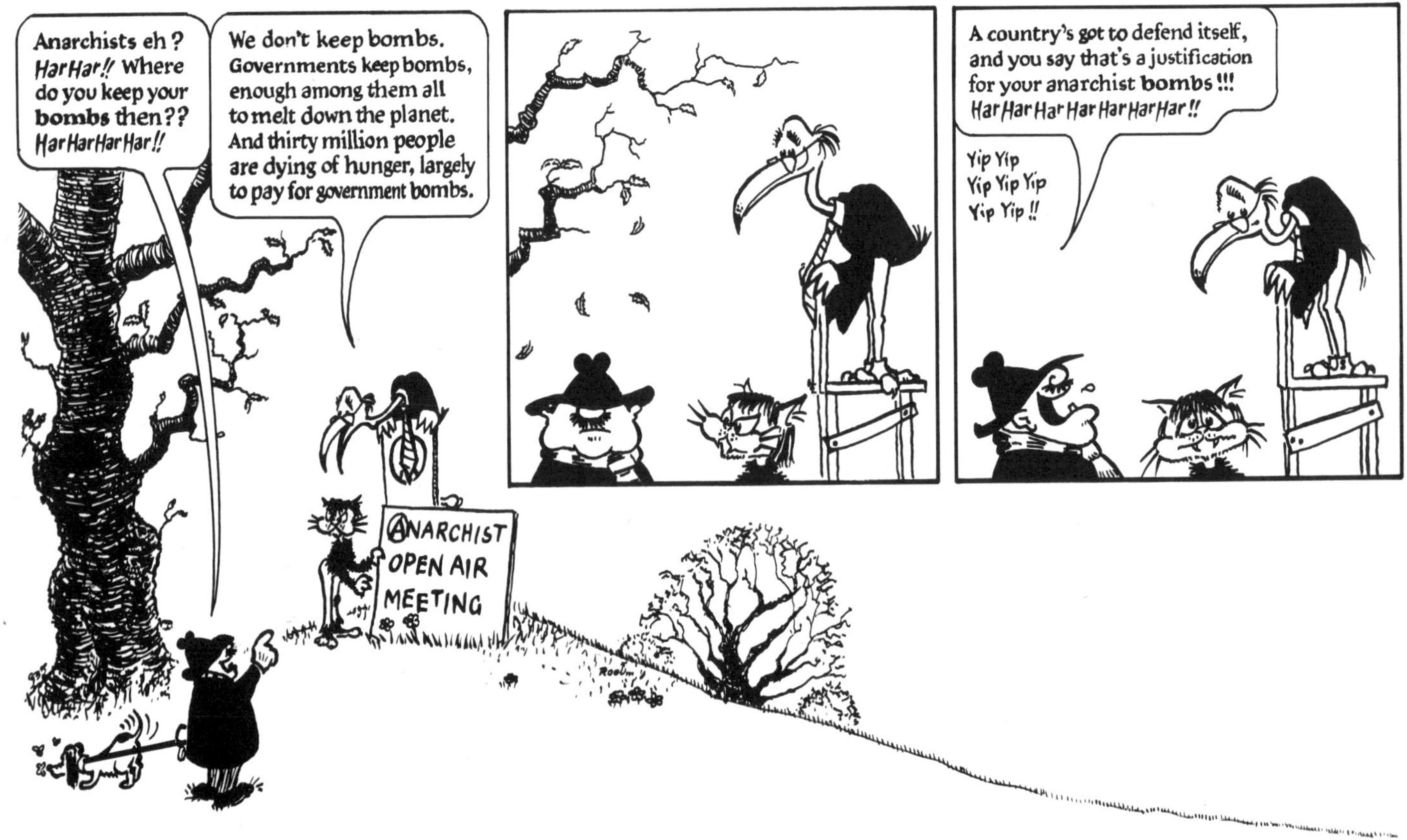

Anarchists eh? HarHar!! Where do you keep your bombs then?? HarHarHarHar!!
We don't keep bombs. Governments keep bombs, enough among them all to melt down the planet. And thirty million people are dying of hunger, largely to pay for government bombs.
ANARCHIST OPEN AIR MEETING
A country's got to defend itself, and you say that's a justification for your anarchist bombs!!! HarHarHarHarHarHarHar!!
Yip Yip Yip Yip Yip Yip Yip!!

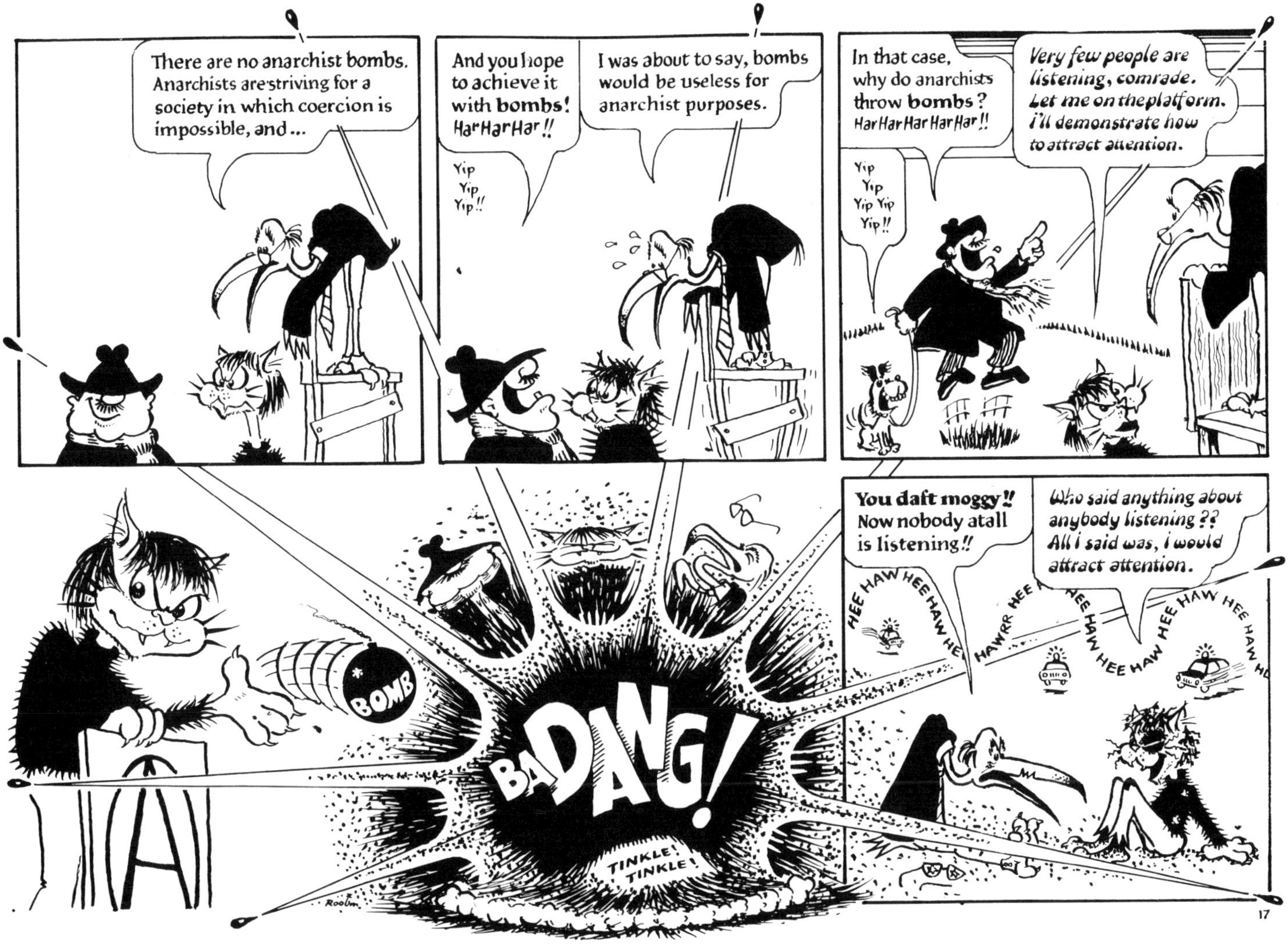
There are no anarchist bombs. Anarchists are striving for a society in which coercion is impossible, and...
And you hope to achieve it with bombs! HarHarHar!!
Yip Yip Yip!!
I was about to say, bombs would be useless for anarchist purposes.
In that case, why do anarchists throw bombs? HarHarHarHarHar!!
Yip Yip Yip Yip Yip!!
Very few people are listening, comrade. Let me on the platform. I'll demonstrate how to attract attention.
BOMB
BADANG!
TINKLE! TINKLE!
You daft moggy!! Now nobody atall is listening!!
Who said anything about anybody listening?? All I said was, I would attract attention.
HEE HAW HEE HAW HEE HAWRR HEE HAW HEE HAW HEE HAW HEE HAW HEE HAW HEE HAW
Roobm

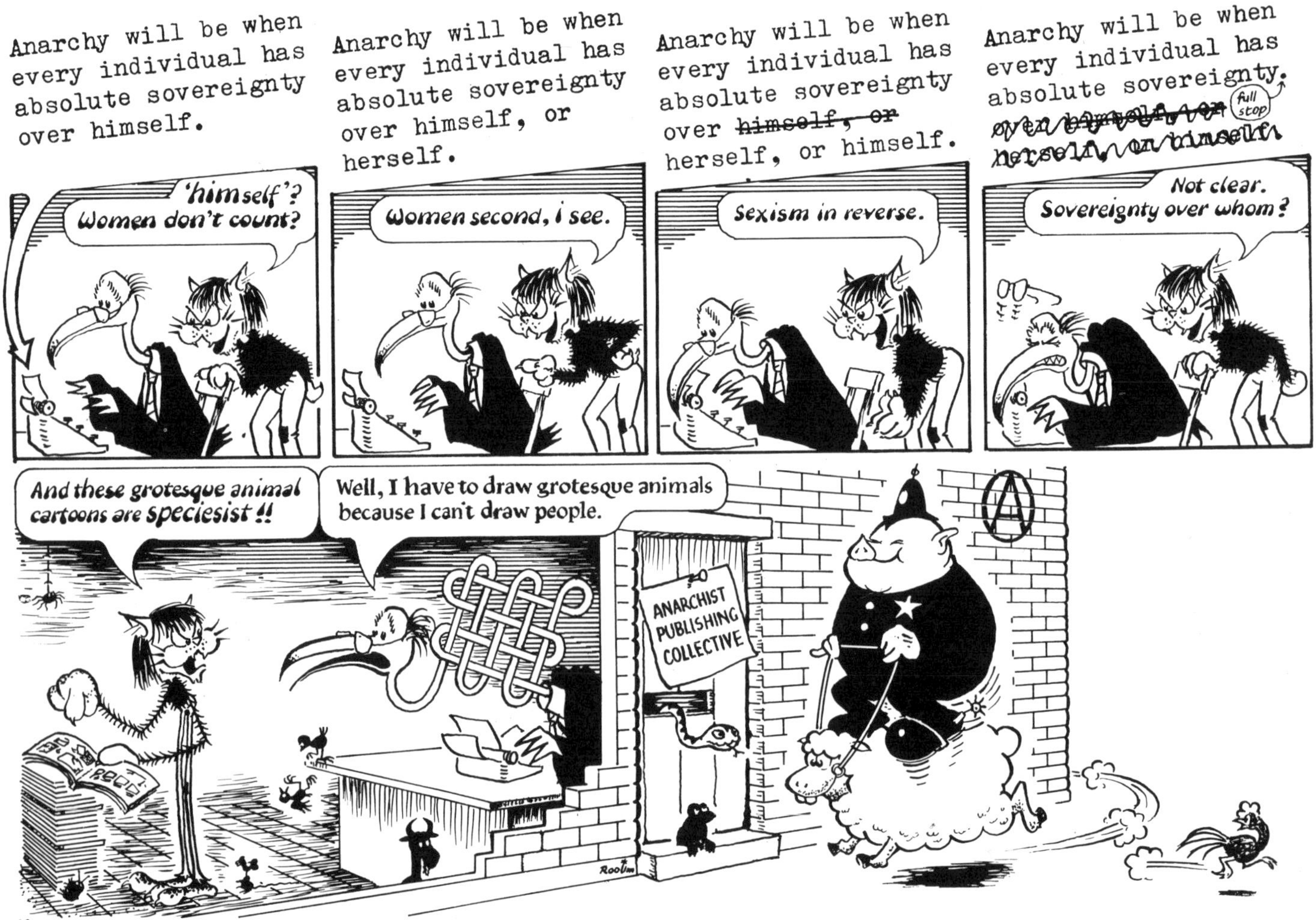
Anarchy will be when every individual has absolute sovereignty over himself.
'himself'? Women don't count?
Anarchy will be when every individual has absolute sovereignty over himself, or herself.
Women second, I see.
Anarchy will be when every individual has absolute sovereignty over ~~himself, or~~ herself, or himself.
Sexism in reverse.
Anarchy will be when every individual has absolute sovereignty. full stop
Not clear. Sovereignty over whom?
And these grotesque animal cartoons are speciesist !!
Well, I have to draw grotesque animals because I can't draw people.
ANARCHIST PUBLISHING COLLECTIVE
Rooum

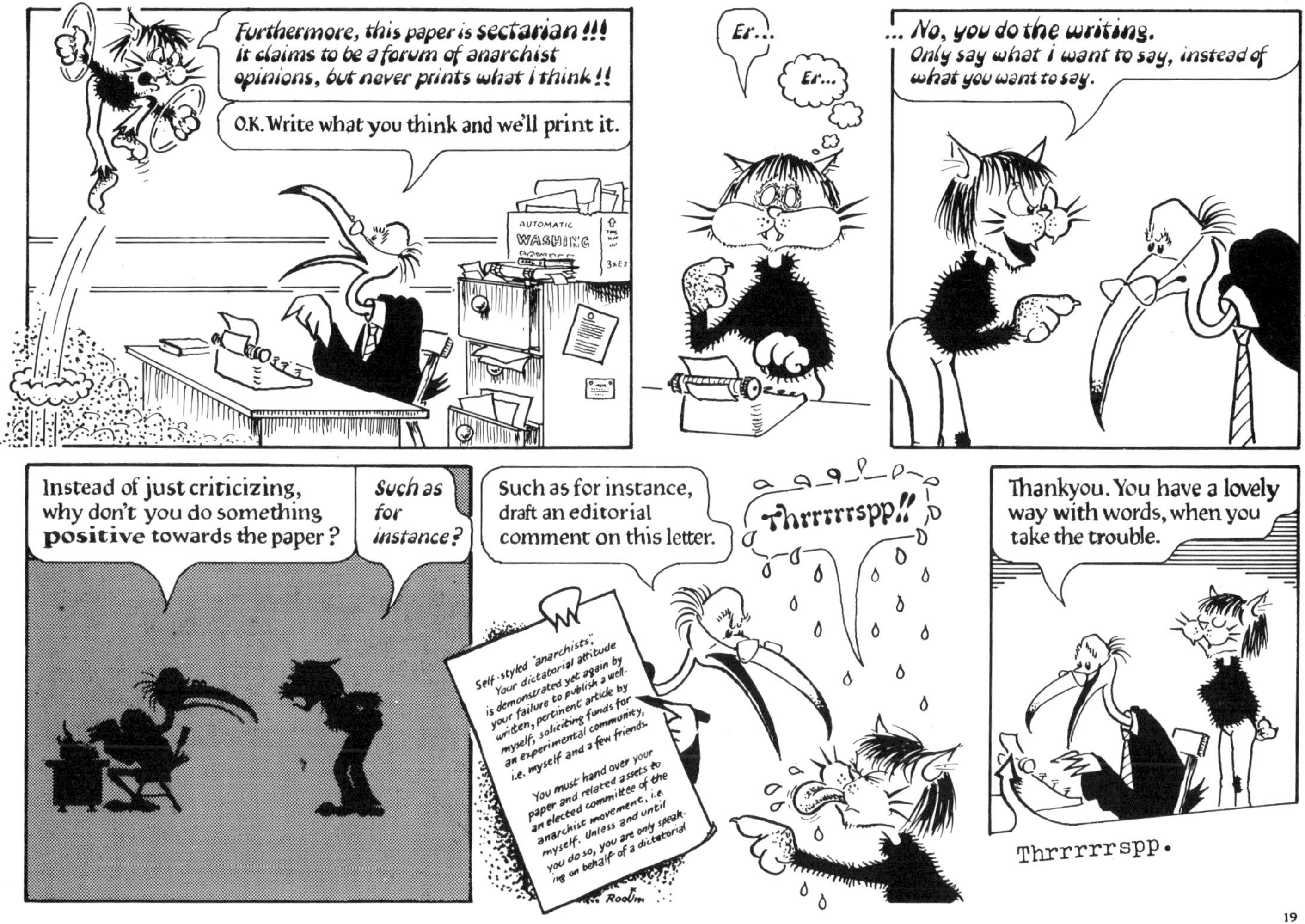
Furthermore, this paper is sectarian !!! It claims to be a forum of anarchist opinions, but never prints what I think !!
O.K. Write what you think and we'll print it.
AUTOMATIC WASHING
Er...
Er...
... No, you do the writing. Only say what I want to say, instead of what you want to say.
Instead of just criticizing, why don't you do something positive towards the paper ?
Such as for instance ?
Such as for instance, draft an editorial comment on this letter.
Self-styled "anarchists", Your dictatorial attitude is demonstrated yet again by your failure to publish a well-written, pertinent article by myself, soliciting funds for an experimental community, i.e. myself and a few friends.
You must hand over your paper and related assets to an elected committee of the anarchist movement, i.e. myself. Unless and until you do so, you are only speaking on behalf of a dictatorial
Roolm
Thrrrrrspp!!
Thankyou. You have a lovely way with words, when you take the trouble.
Thrrrrrspp.

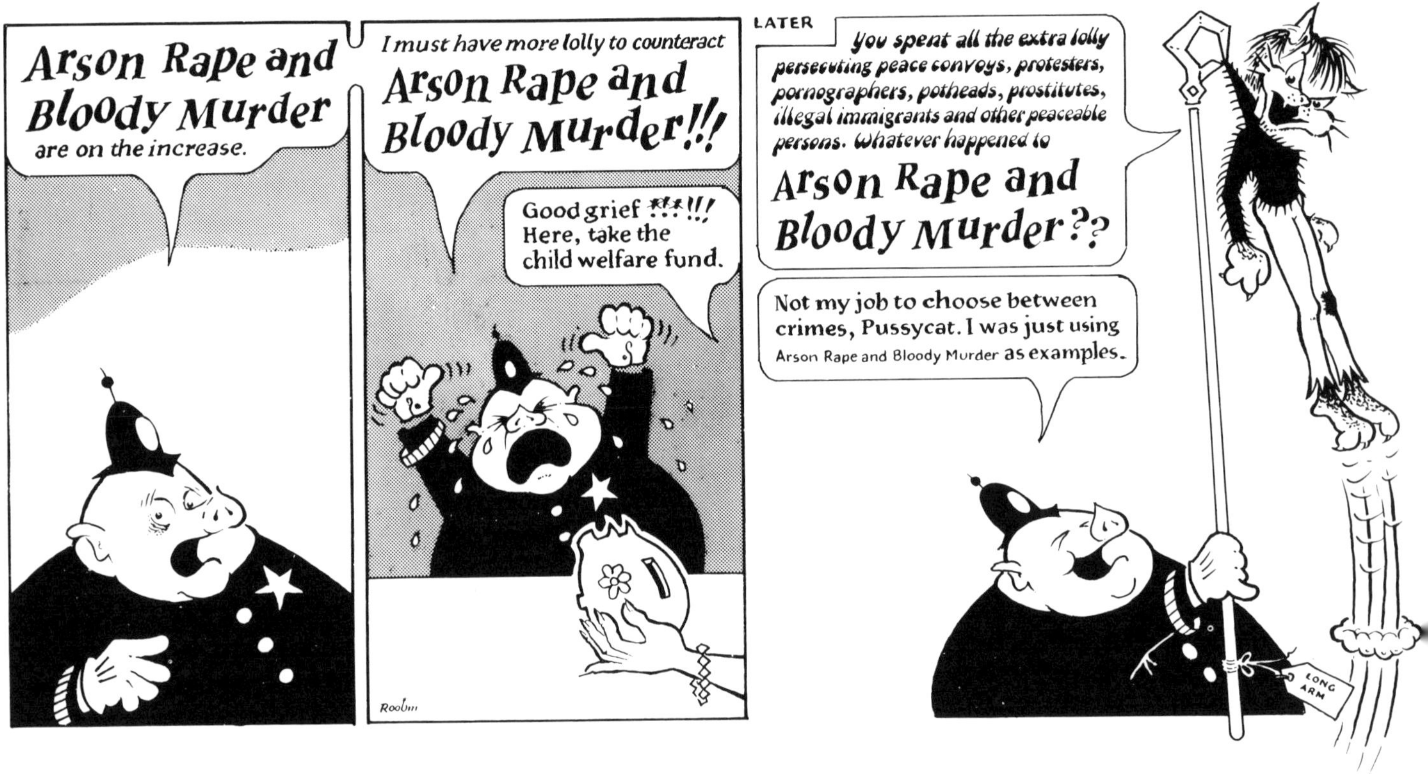
Arson Rape and Bloody Murder are on the increase.
I must have more lolly to counteract Arson Rape and Bloody Murder!!!
Good grief !!!
Here, take the child welfare fund.
Roobin
LATER
You spent all the extra lolly persecuting peace convoys, protesters, pornographers, potheads, prostitutes, illegal immigrants and other peaceable persons. Whatever happened to Arson Rape and Bloody Murder??
Not my job to choose between crimes, Pussycat. I was just using Arson Rape and Bloody Murder as examples.
LONG ARM

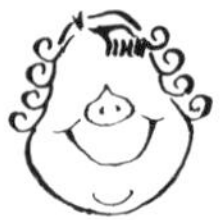

SUPERFLUOUS EXPLANATION. As readers will have noticed, our "policeman" embodies a rebus or visual pun on the surname of England's foremost law officer, the Lord Chancellor, Quintin Hogg.

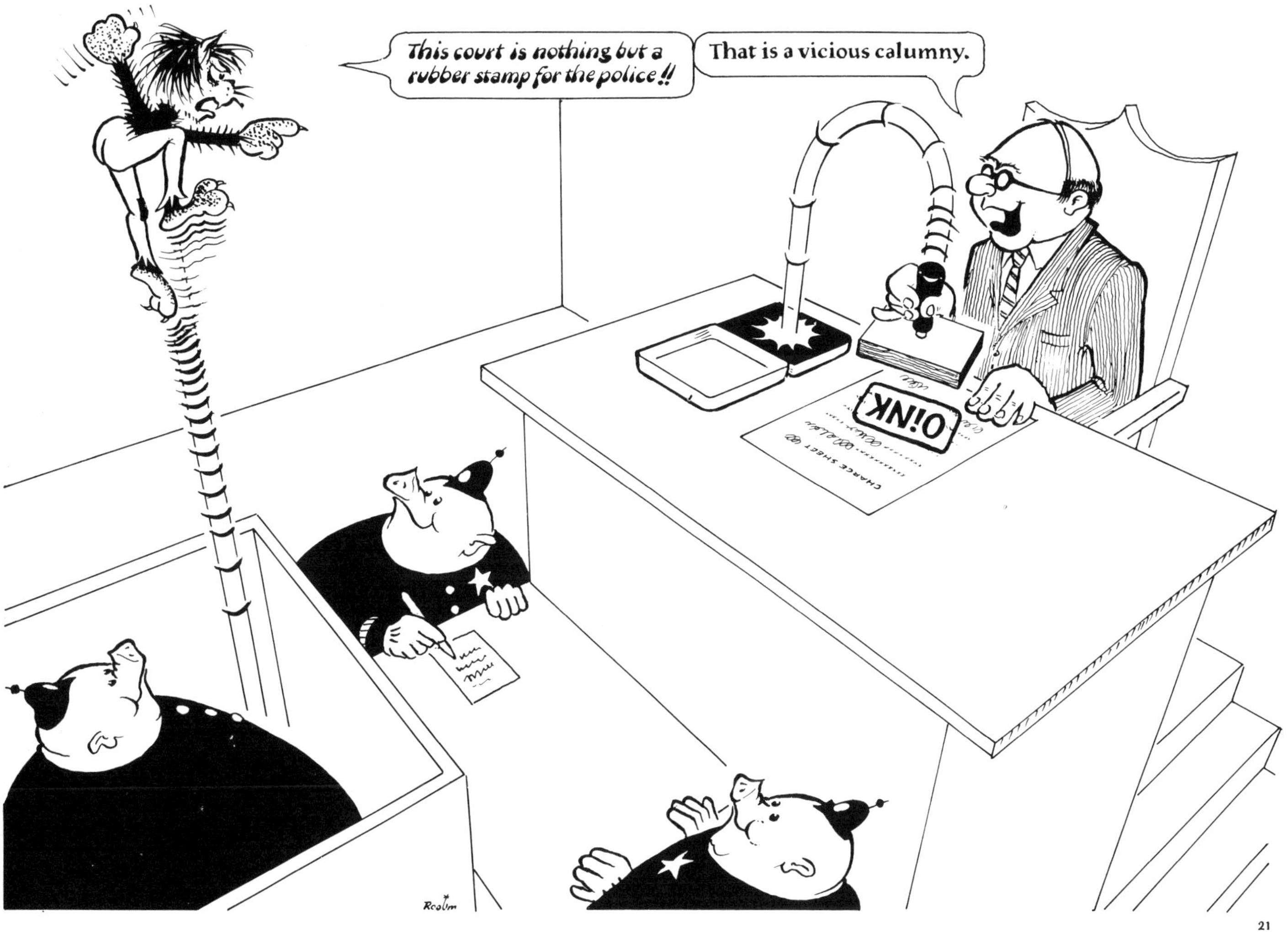
This court is nothing but a rubber stamp for the police!!
That is a vicious calumny.
OiNK
CHARGE SHEET

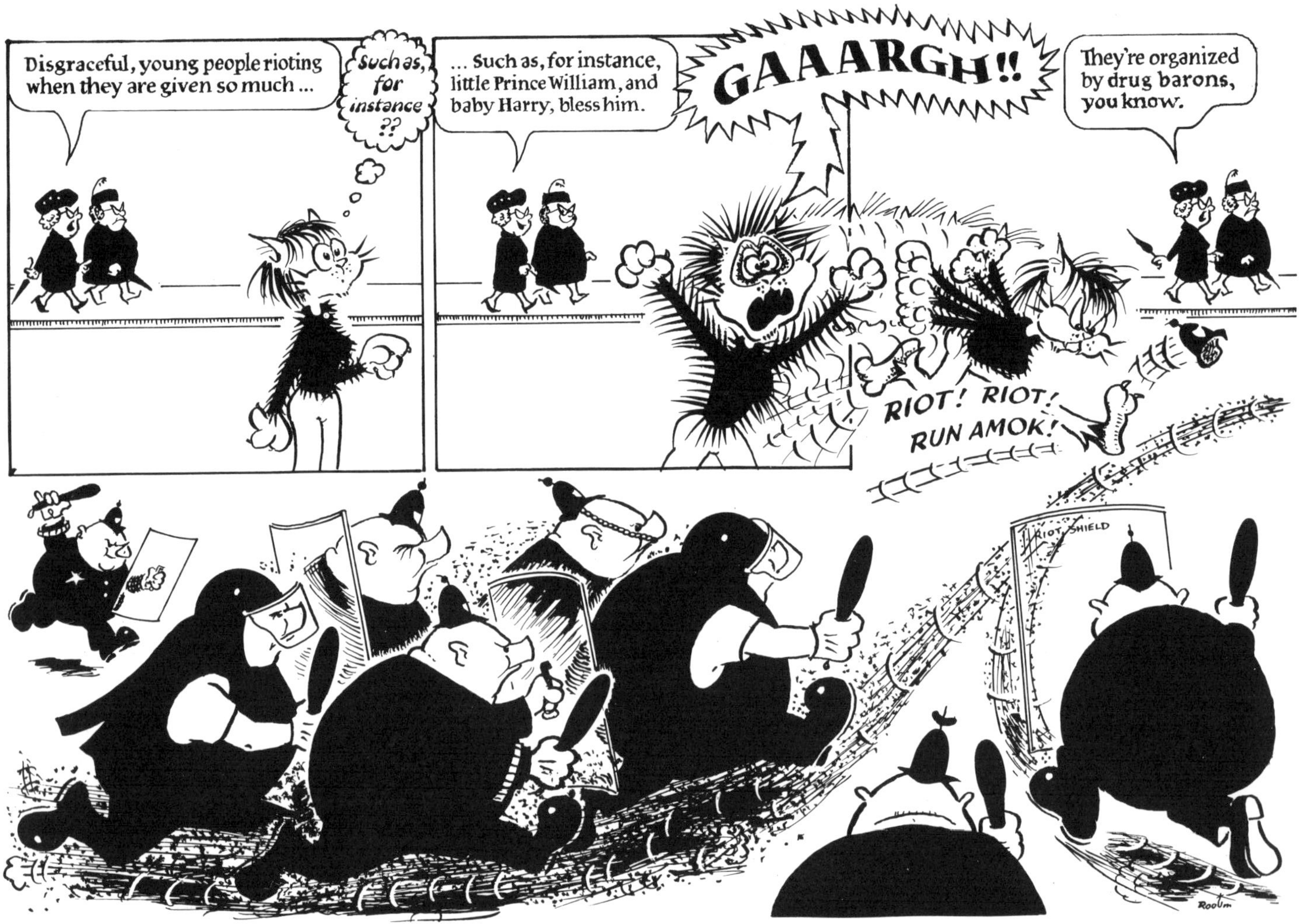

Disgraceful, young people rioting when they are given so much ...
Such as, for instance ??
... Such as, for instance, little Prince William, and baby Harry, bless him.
GAAARGH!!
They're organized by drug barons, you know.
RIOT! RIOT! RUN AMOK!
RIOT SHIELD
ROOTUM

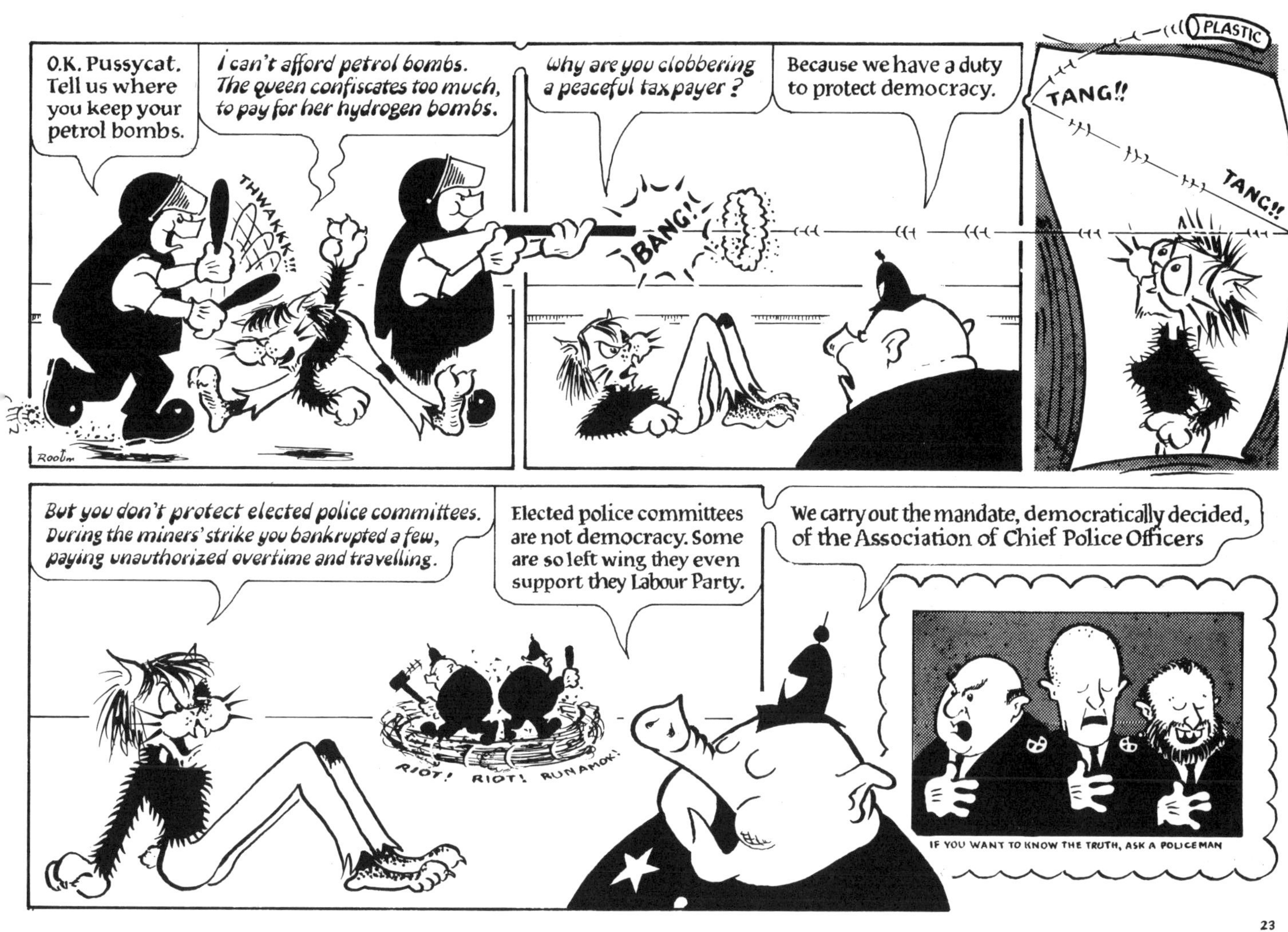
O.K. Pussycat. Tell us where you keep your petrol bombs.
I can't afford petrol bombs. The queen confiscates too much, to pay for her hydrogen bombs.
THWAKKK!!!
Why are you clobbering a peaceful tax payer ?
Because we have a duty to protect democracy.
BANG!!
PLASTIC
TANG!!
TANG!!
But you don't protect elected police committees. During the miners' strike you bankrupted a few, paying unauthorized overtime and travelling.
Elected police committees are not democracy. Some are so left wing they even support they Labour Party.
RIOT! RIOT! RUN AMOK!
We carry out the mandate, democratically decided, of the Association of Chief Police Officers
IF YOU WANT TO KNOW THE TRUTH, ASK A POLICEMAN

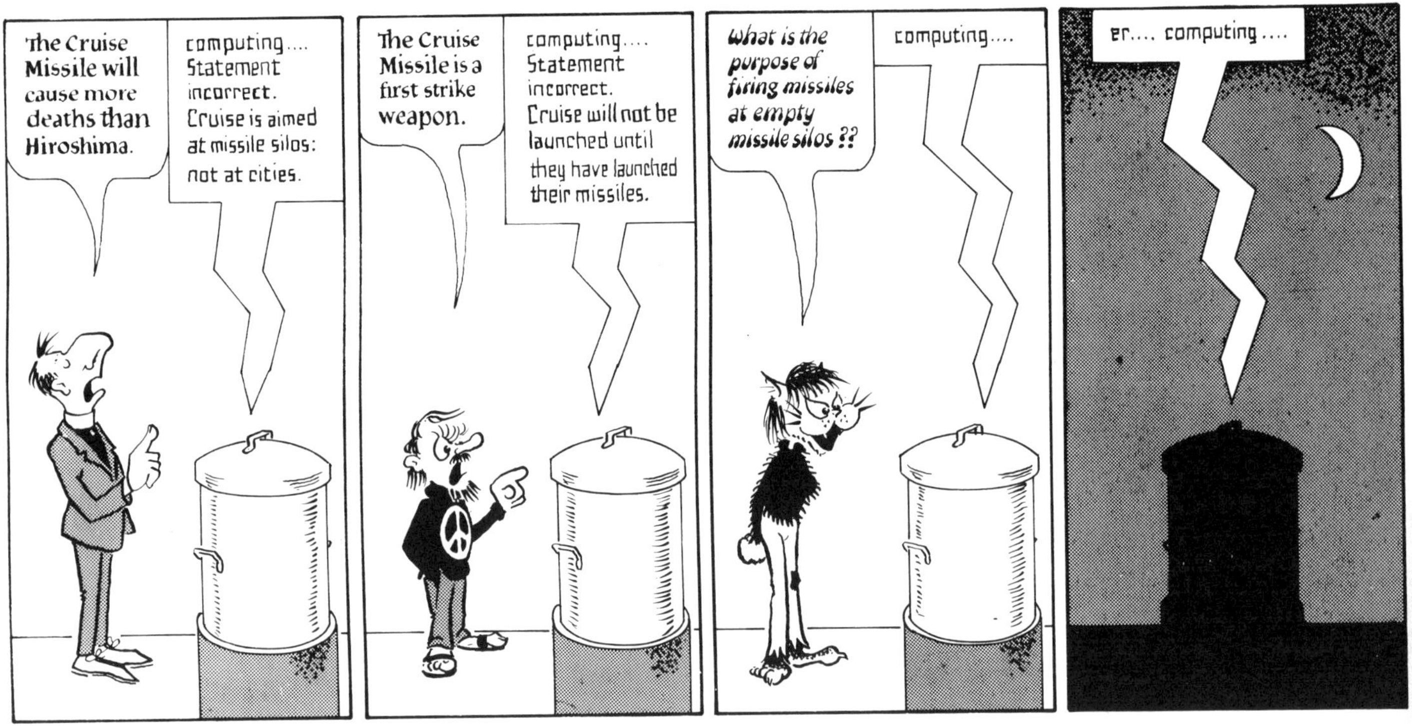
The Cruise Missile will cause more deaths than Hiroshima.
computing.... Statement incorrect. Cruise is aimed at missile silos: not at cities.
The Cruise Missile is a first strike weapon.
computing.... Statement incorrect. Cruise will not be launched until they have launched their missiles.
What is the purpose of firing missiles at empty missile silos ??
computing....
er.... computing....

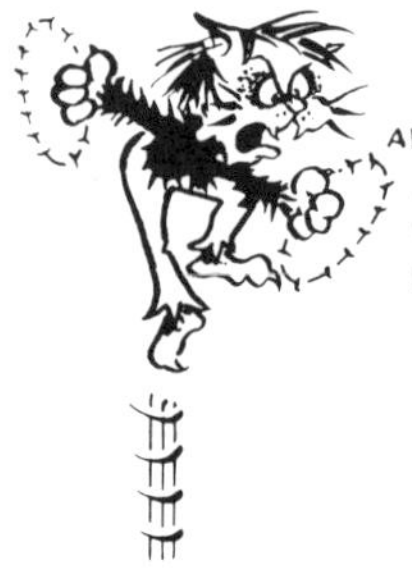

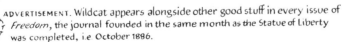

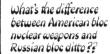

What's the difference between American bloc nuclear weapons and Russian bloc ditto??

computing..... Ours are solely for defence. Theirs are for taking up aggressive postures.

Is that the Nato think tank, or the Warsaw Pact think tank?

Dunno. you can't tell them apart, if you can't see the label.

Correct. We have a joint policy to preserve peace by the threat of mutual destruction.

NUCLEAR DEFENCE THINK TANK

What a bloody dangerous policy !!! Why don't you stop the arms race??

  You have three guesses.

Governments need external enemies to keep their own subjects in order?

 Guess one: incorrect.

If politicians cut down on weaponry, the military would take over?

 Guess two: incorrect.

There's only one other possibility...

 Guess three: correct.

Guess three correct. Guess three correct. **Guess three correct.** We are Daleks in disguise.

Exterminate

Exterminate

FOOM!!

FROOOOSH!!

FRIZZZZ!!!

HRUNK!!

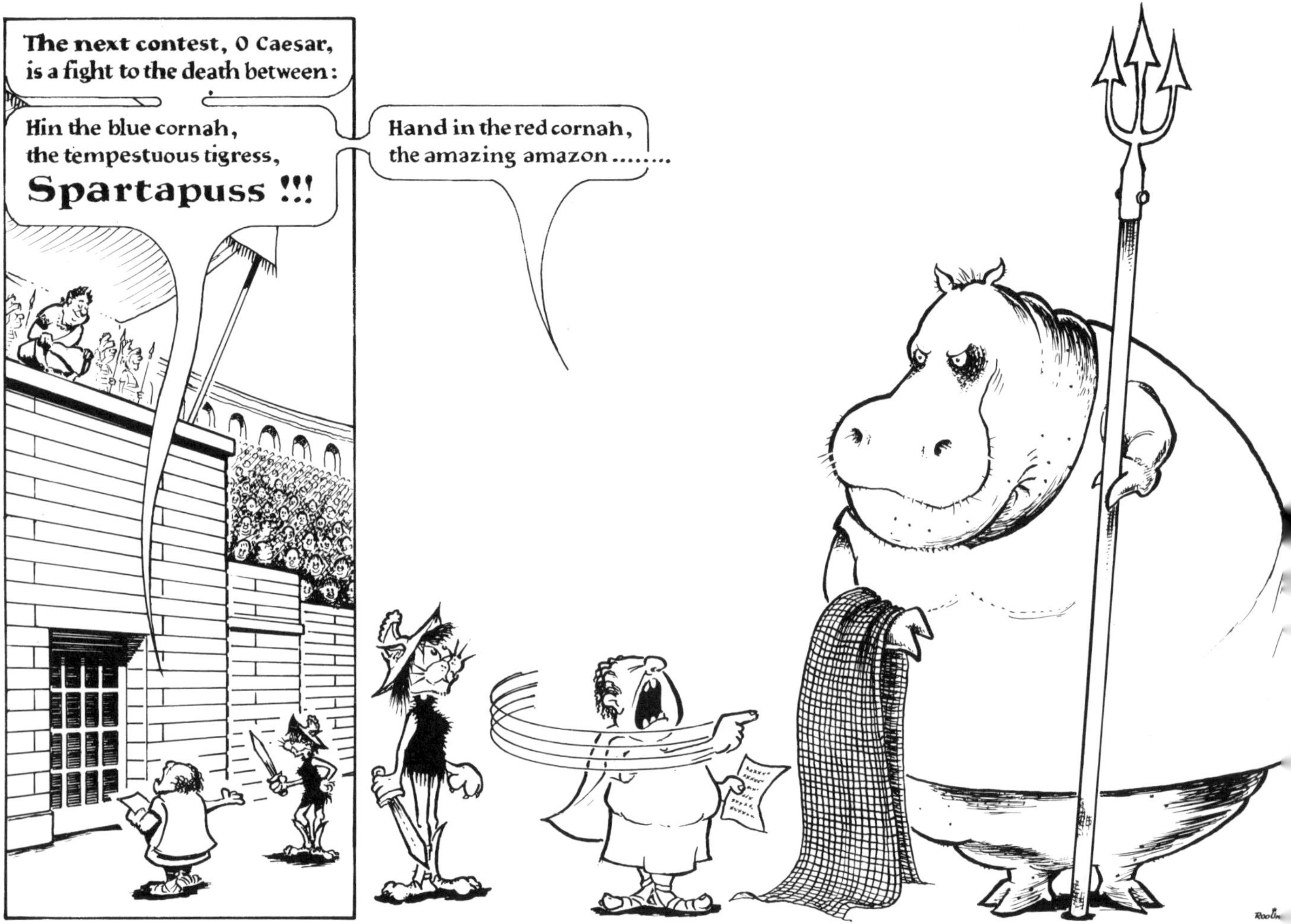
The next contest, O Caesar, is a fight to the death between:
Hin the blue cornah, the tempestuous tigress, Spartapuss !!!
Hand in the red cornah, the amazing amazon ....

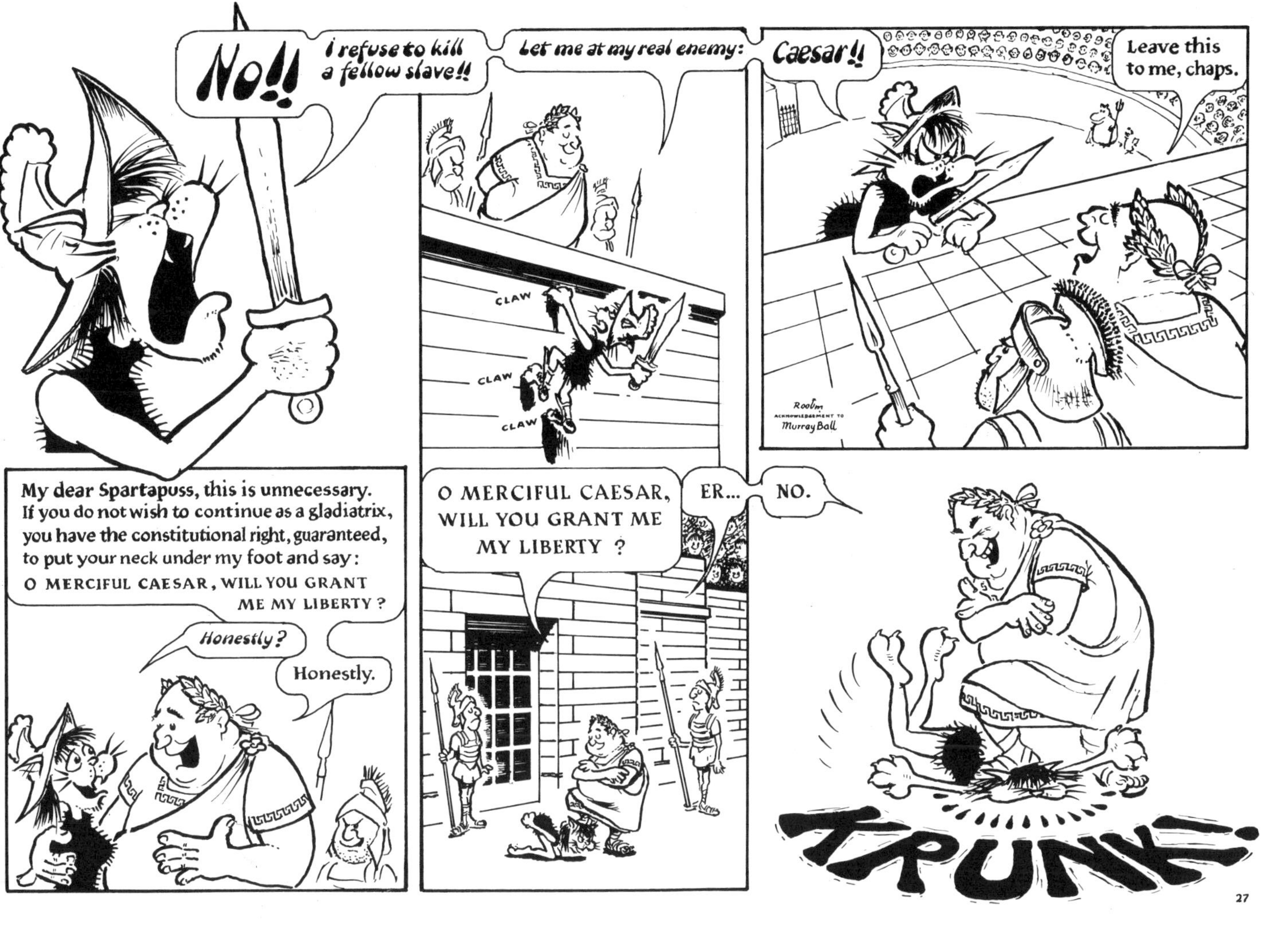
No!!
i refuse to kill a fellow slave!!
Let me at my real enemy:
Caesar!!
Leave this to me, chaps.
CLAW
CLAW
CLAW
Roobm
ACKNOWLEDGEMENT TO
Murray Ball
My dear Spartapuss, this is unnecessary. If you do not wish to continue as a gladiatrix, you have the constitutional right, guaranteed, to put your neck under my foot and say: O MERCIFUL CAESAR, WILL YOU GRANT ME MY LIBERTY ?
Honestly?
Honestly.
O MERCIFUL CAESAR, WILL YOU GRANT ME MY LIBERTY ?
ER...
NO.
TRUNK!

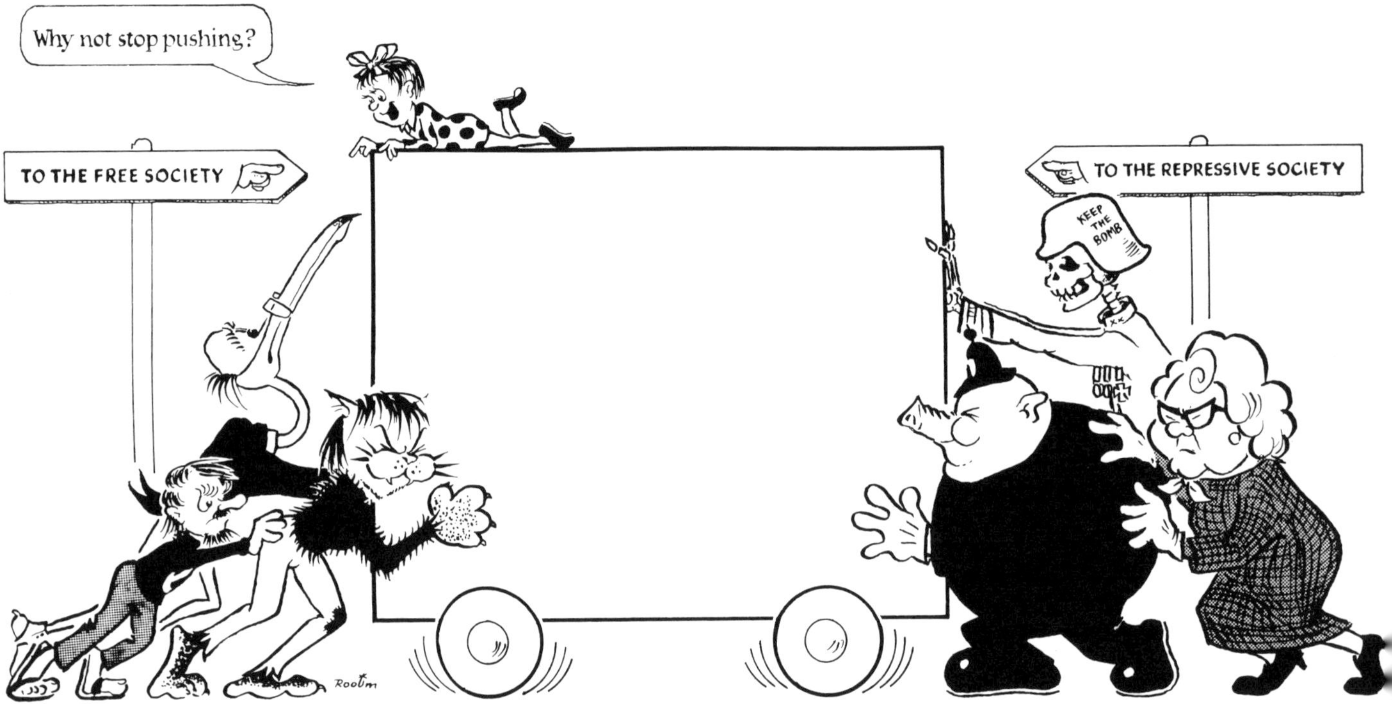
Why not stop pushing?
TO THE FREE SOCIETY
TO THE REPRESSIVE SOCIETY
KEEP THE BOMB
Rooum

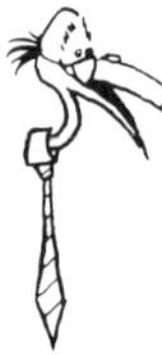

MISQUOTATION. The question of when (or even whether) anarchy will be attained is not important. What is important is that we work towards anarchy. I dare say somebody said that.

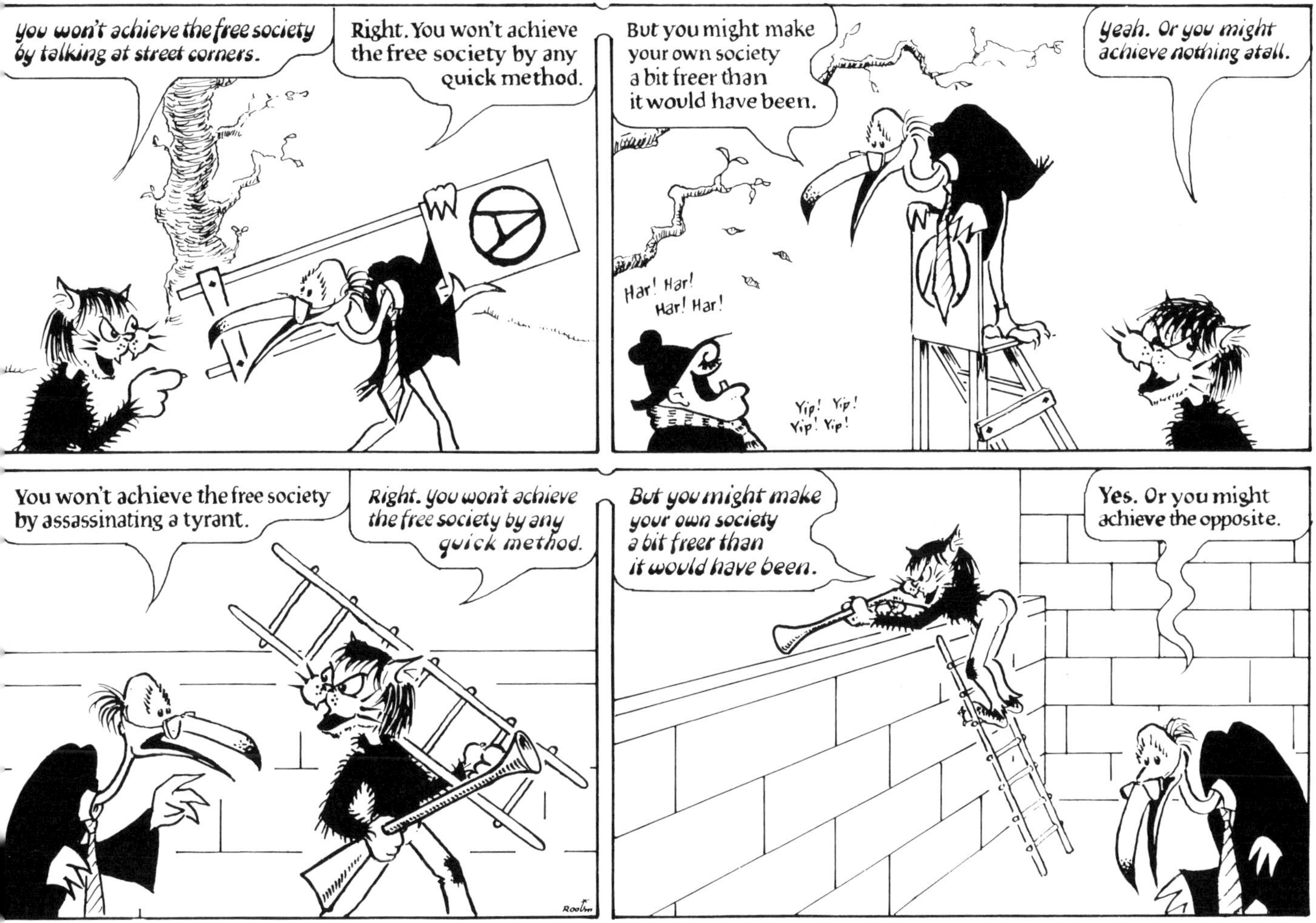
You won't achieve the free society by talking at street corners.
Right. You won't achieve the free society by any quick method.
But you might make your own society a bit freer than it would have been.
Yeah. Or you might achieve nothing atall.
Har! Har! Har! Har!
Yip! Yip! Yip! Yip!
You won't achieve the free society by assassinating a tyrant.
Right. You won't achieve the free society by any quick method.
But you might make your own society a bit freer than it would have been.
Yes. Or you might achieve the opposite.
Rooum

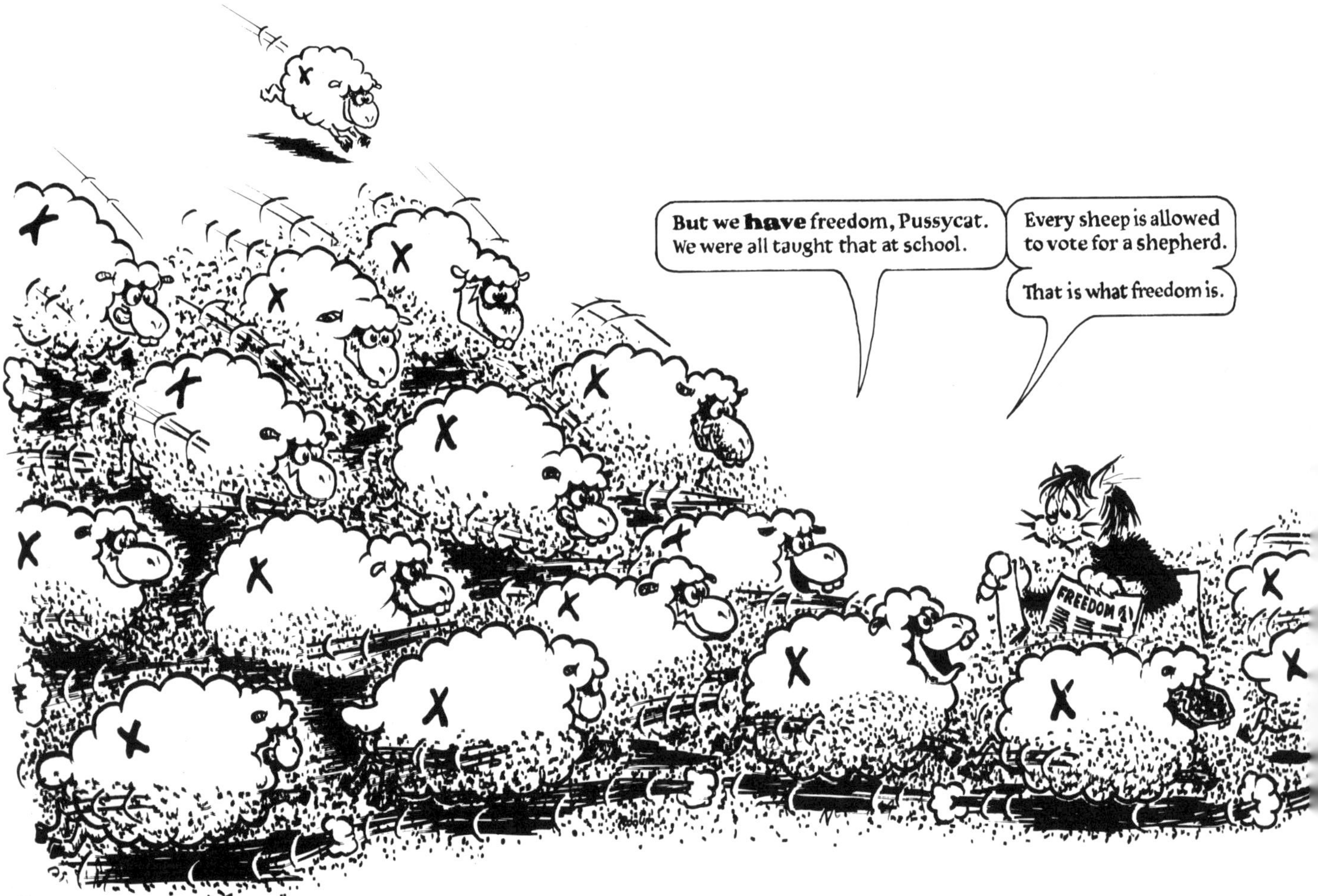
But we **have** freedom, Pussycat. We were all taught that at school.
Every sheep is allowed to vote for a shepherd.
That is what freedom is.
FREEDOM

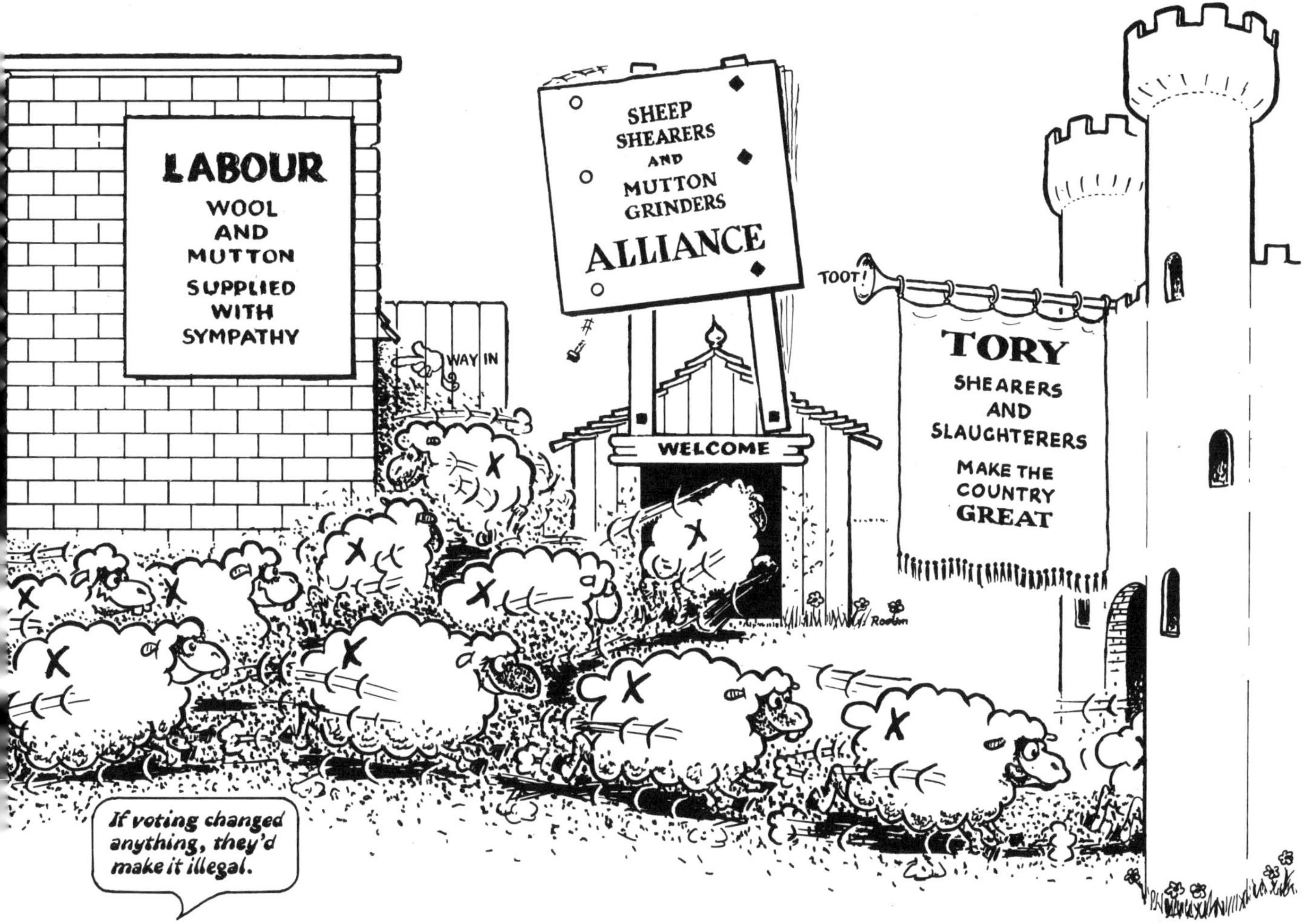
LABOUR
WOOL
AND
MUTTON
SUPPLIED
WITH
SYMPATHY
SHEEP
SHEARERS
AND
MUTTON
GRINDERS
ALLIANCE
WAY IN
WELCOME
TOOT!
TORY
SHEARERS
AND
SLAUGHTERERS
MAKE THE
COUNTRY
GREAT
If voting changed anything, they'd make it illegal.

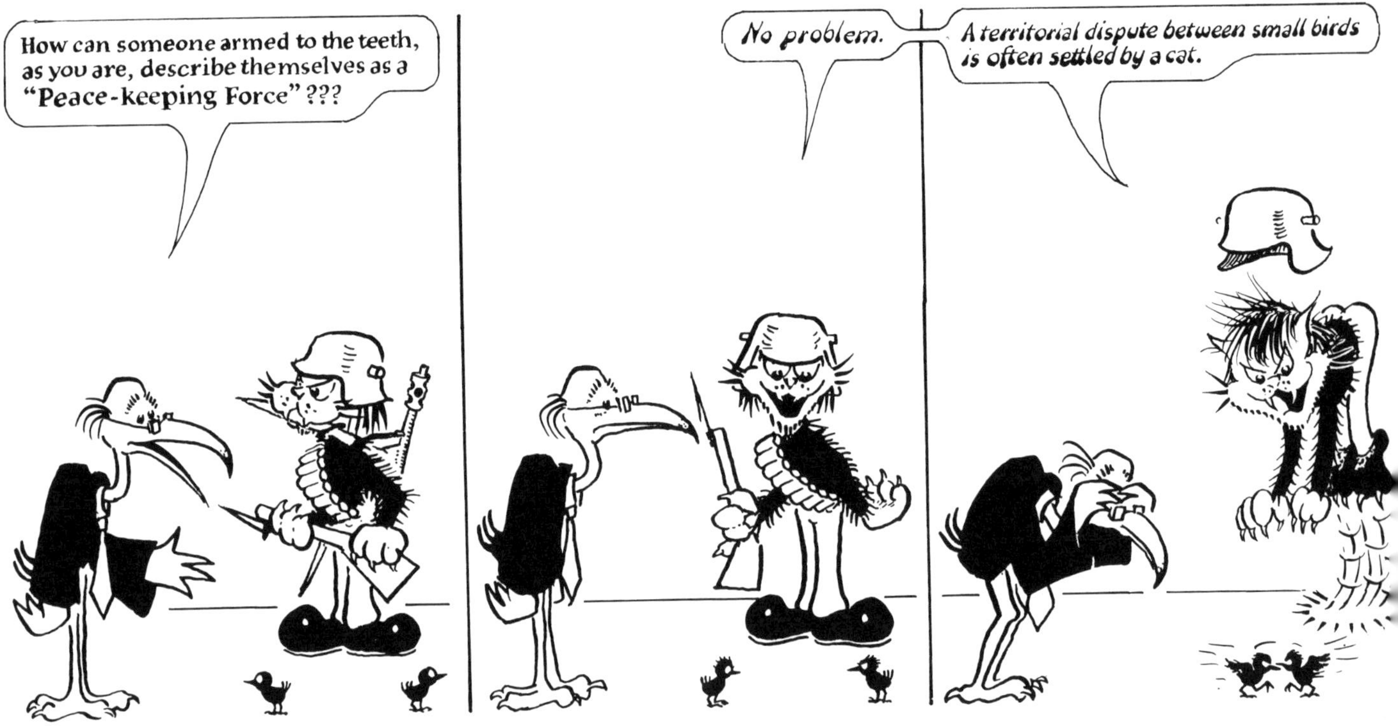
How can someone armed to the teeth, as you are, describe themselves as a "Peace-keeping Force" ???
No problem.
A territorial dispute between small birds is often settled by a cat.

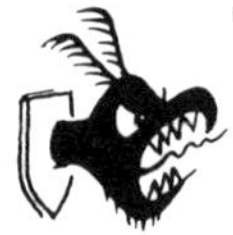

NOT ABOUT THIS PAGE. Or the page opposite. About the two pages following.
A shorter version of the story provoked, among other correspondence, a death threat from a censorian signing herself, or himself, "The Black Dragons".

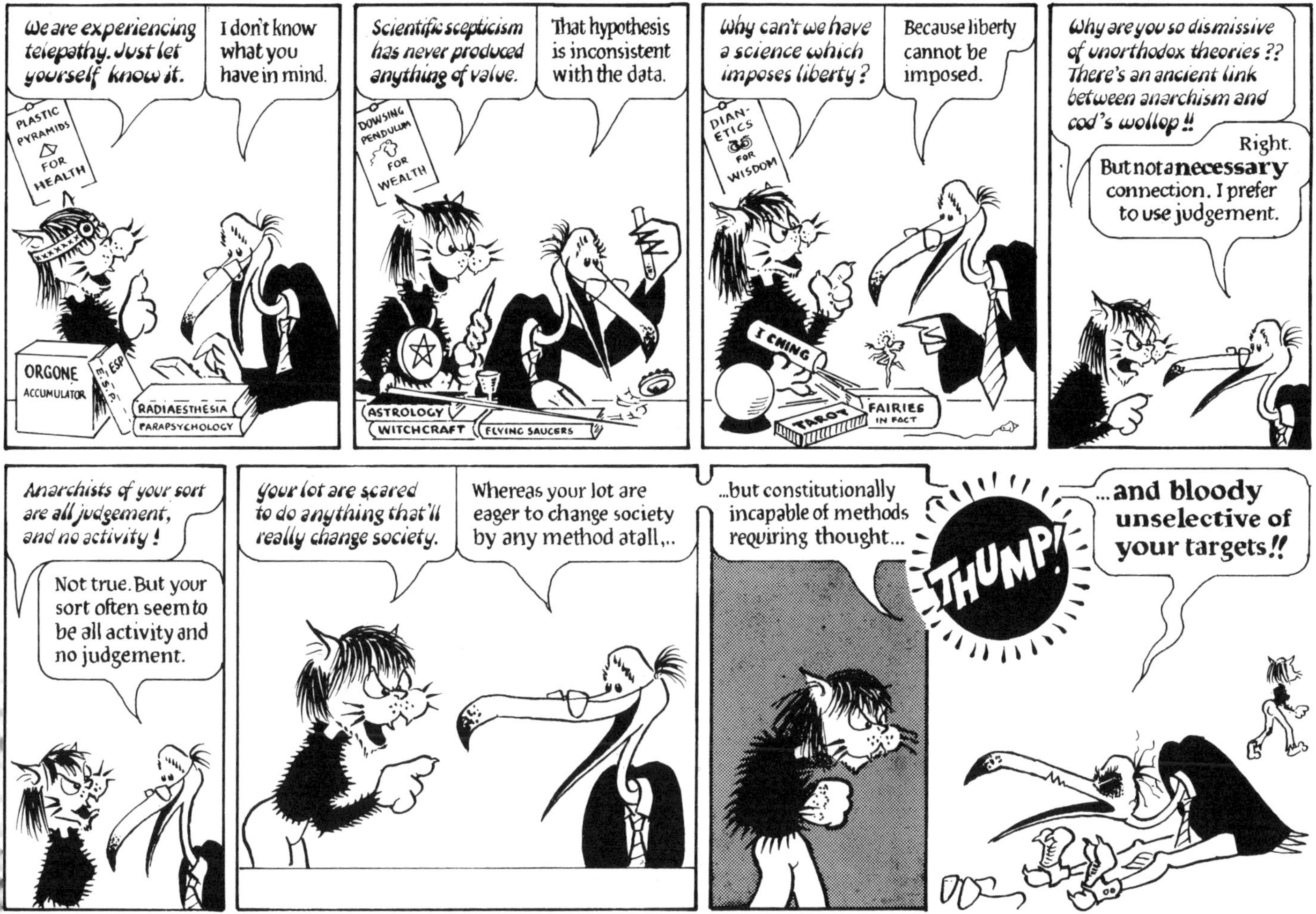
We are experiencing telepathy. Just let yourself know it.
I don't know what you have in mind.
PLASTIC PYRAMIDS FOR HEALTH
ORGONE ACCUMULATOR
E.S.P.
ESP
RADIAESTHESIA
PARAPSYCHOLOGY
Scientific scepticism has never produced anything of value.
That hypothesis is inconsistent with the data.
DOWSING PENDULUM FOR WEALTH
ASTROLOGY
WITCHCRAFT
FLYING SAUCERS
Why can't we have a science which imposes liberty?
Because liberty cannot be imposed.
DIAN-ETICS FOR WISDOM
I CHING
TAROT
FAIRIES IN FACT
Why are you so dismissive of unorthodox theories ?? There's an ancient link between anarchism and cod's wollop !!
Right. But not a **necessary** connection. I prefer to use judgement.
Anarchists of your sort are all judgement, and no activity !
Not true. But your sort often seem to be all activity and no judgement.
Your lot are scared to do anything that'll really change society.
Whereas your lot are eager to change society by any method atall,..
...but constitutionally incapable of methods requiring thought...
THUMP!
...**and bloody unselective of your targets!!**

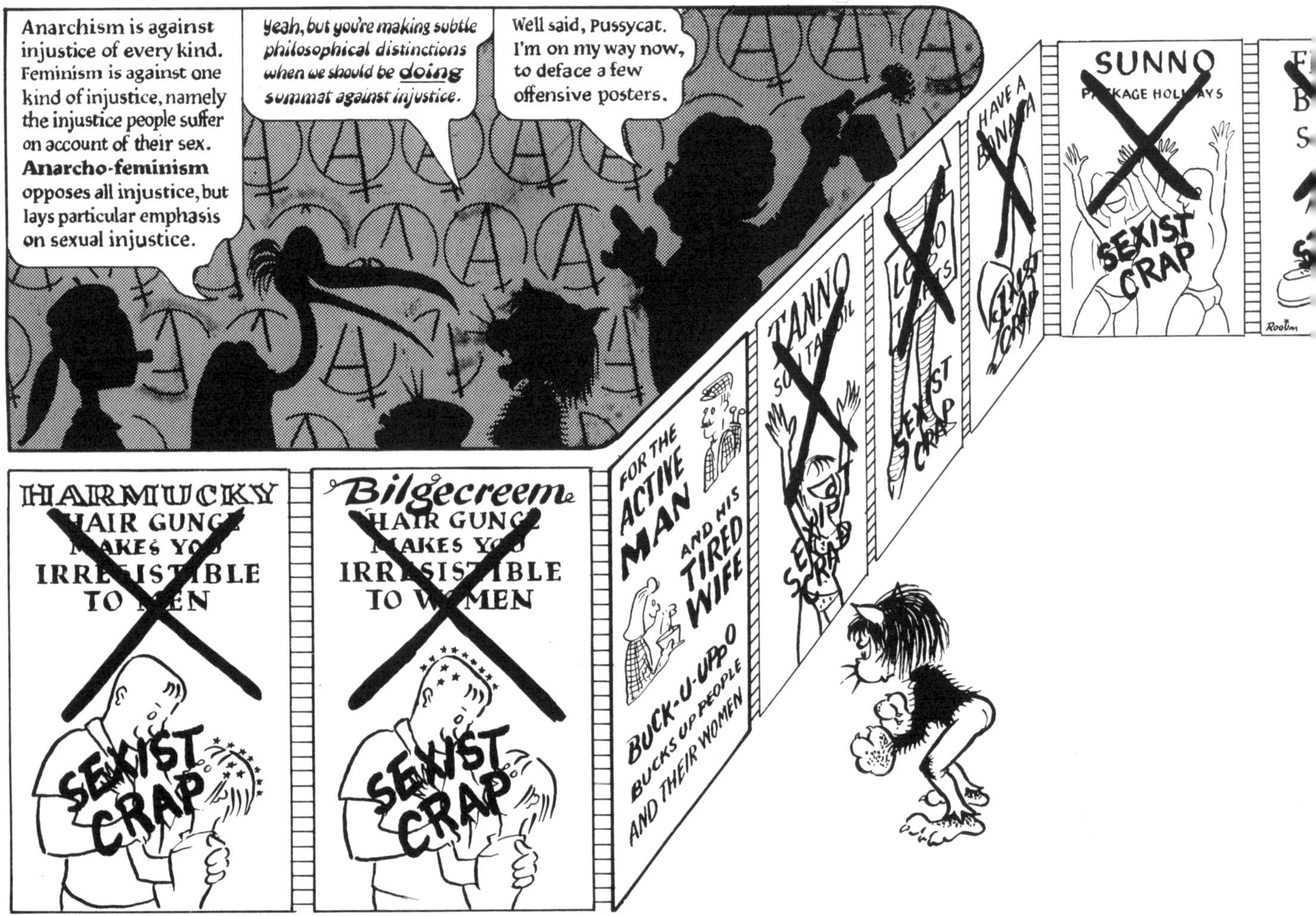

Anarchism is against injustice of every kind. Feminism is against one kind of injustice, namely the injustice people suffer on account of their sex. **Anarcho-feminism** opposes all injustice, but lays particular emphasis on sexual injustice.
Yeah, but you're making subtle philosophical distinctions when we should be doing summat against injustice.
Well said, Pussycat. I'm on my way now, to deface a few offensive posters.
SUNNO
PACKAGE HOLIDAYS
SEXIST CRAP
HAVE A
SEXIST CRAP
SEXIST CRAP
TANNO
SEXIST CRAP
FOR THE ACTIVE MAN
AND HIS TIRED WIFE
BUCK-U-UPPO
BUCKS UP PEOPLE AND THEIR WOMEN
HARMUCKY
HAIR GUNGE MAKES YOU IRRESISTIBLE TO MEN
SEXIST CRAP
Bilgecreem
HAIR GUNGE MAKES YOU IRRESISTIBLE TO WOMEN
SEXIST CRAP
Rooum

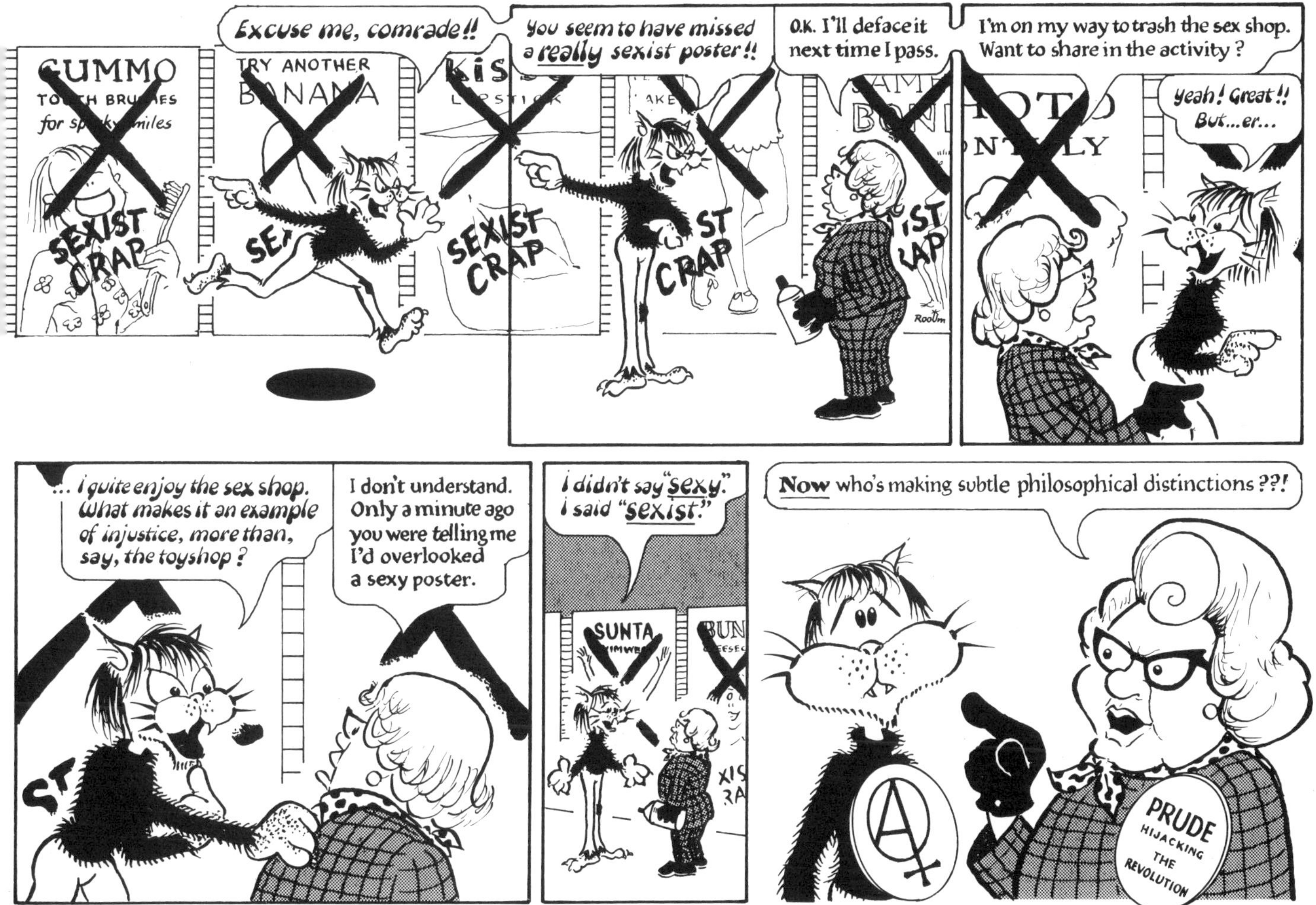
Excuse me, comrade!!
You seem to have missed a really sexist poster!!
O.K. I'll deface it next time I pass.
I'm on my way to trash the sex shop. Want to share in the activity ?
Yeah! Great!! But...er...
... i quite enjoy the sex shop. What makes it an example of injustice, more than, say, the toyshop ?
I don't understand. Only a minute ago you were telling me I'd overlooked a sexy poster.
i didn't say "sexy." i said "sexist."
Now who's making subtle philosophical distinctions ??!
TRY ANOTHER
SEXIST CRAP
PRUDE HIJACKING THE REVOLUTION

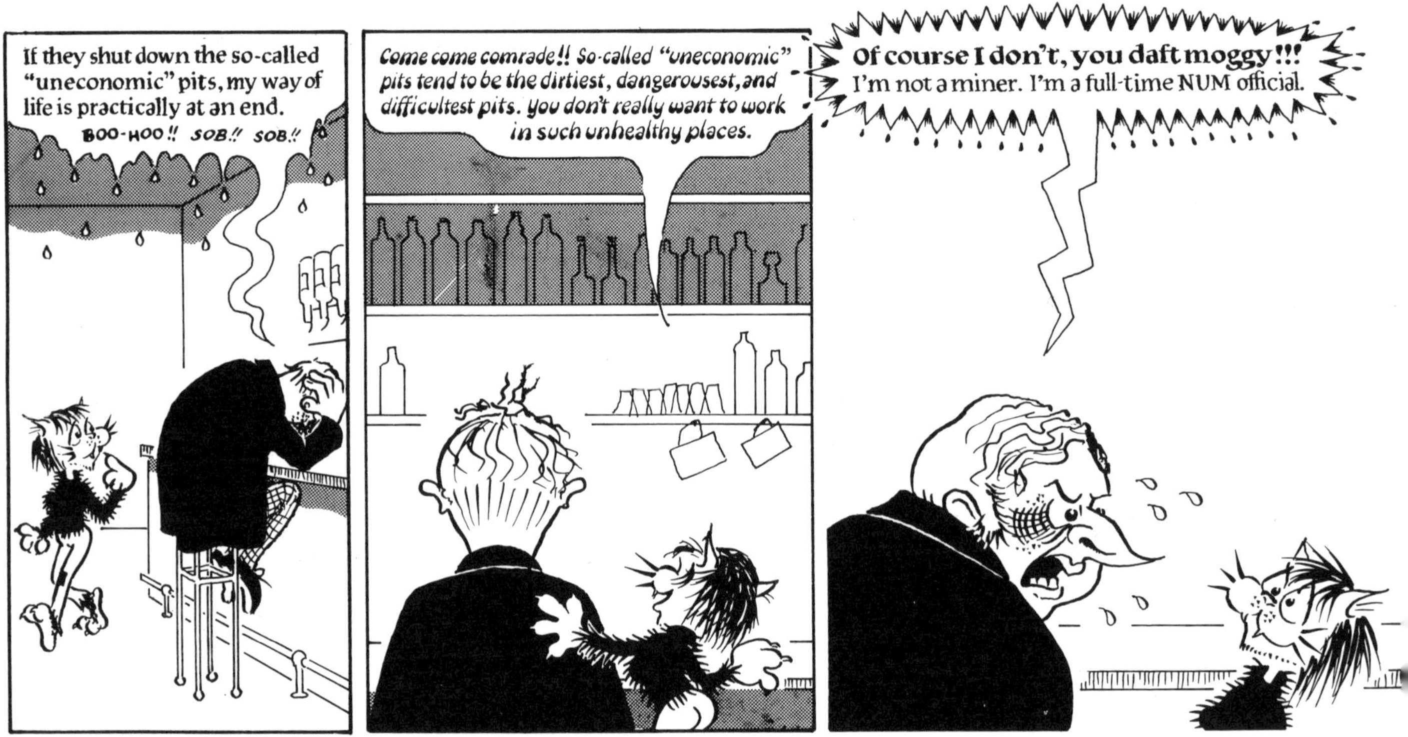
If they shut down the so-called "uneconomic" pits, my way of life is practically at an end.
BOO-HOO!! SOB!! SOB!!
Come come comrade!! So-called "uneconomic" pits tend to be the dirtiest, dangerousest, and difficultest pits. You don't really want to work in such unhealthy places.
Of course I don't, you daft moggy!!! I'm not a miner. I'm a full-time NUM official.

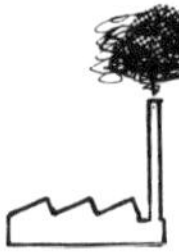

CHANGE OF MIND. When I was little, Sundays in Bradford were brighter than other days. I thought at the time this was due to the weekly concentration of prayer, but now I think it was because the mills stopped burning coal at week ends.

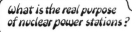

What is the real purpose of nuclear power stations?

C.E.G.B.

QUESTIONS ON NUCLEAR POWER ANSWERED HERE

BUZZ CRACKLE Well for a start there is no question of them generating weapons grade plutonium those which already do so are beyond our jurisdiction it is irrelevant that we distribute the electricity they produce through the national grid nor is it envisaged that nuclear fuel will replace other sources of energy the fact is that in this nuclear age we use more and more energy a great deal is used for instance in building nuclear power stations to exacting standards of precision and of course safety also expensive in energy terms is the extraction and refinement of uranium from pitchblende and above all the disposal of radioactive waste which has to be transported in heavy but exactly made containers and deposited where the radio-

Sometimes i wonder whether i've been brainwashed.

Er... Nobody actually **died** at Three Mile Island.

nuclear power out

REMEMBER THE DEAD OF THREE MILE ISLAND

COAL NOT NUKES

NO NUKES

COAL LOBBY

REMEMBER THE DEAD OF

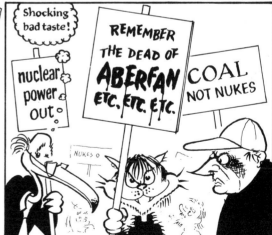

Shocking bad taste!

nuclear power out

REMEMBER THE DEAD OF ABERFAN ETC. ETC. ETC.

COAL NOT NUKES

NUKES O

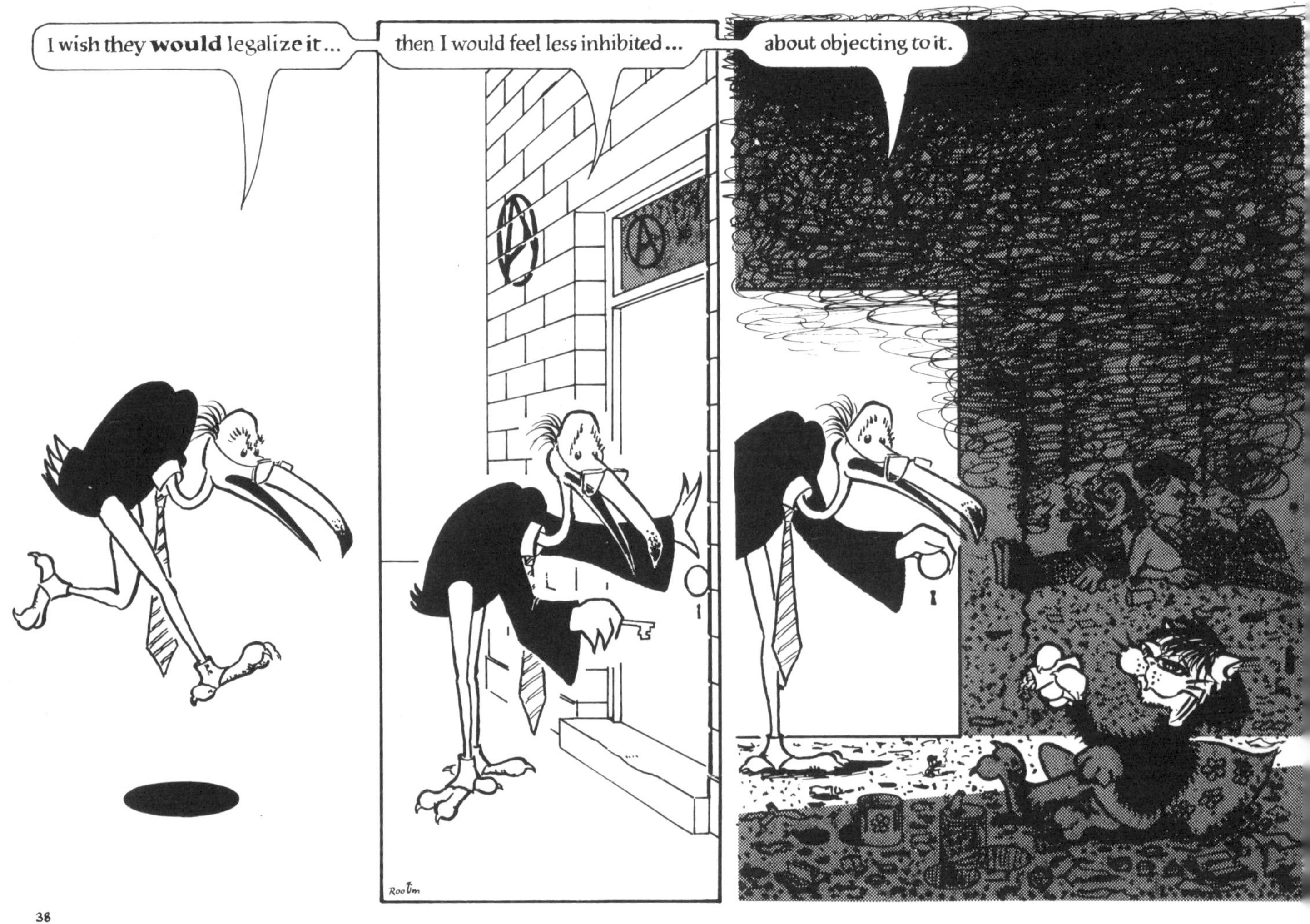
I wish they **would** legalize **it** ...
then I would feel less inhibited ...
about objecting to it.
Rootin

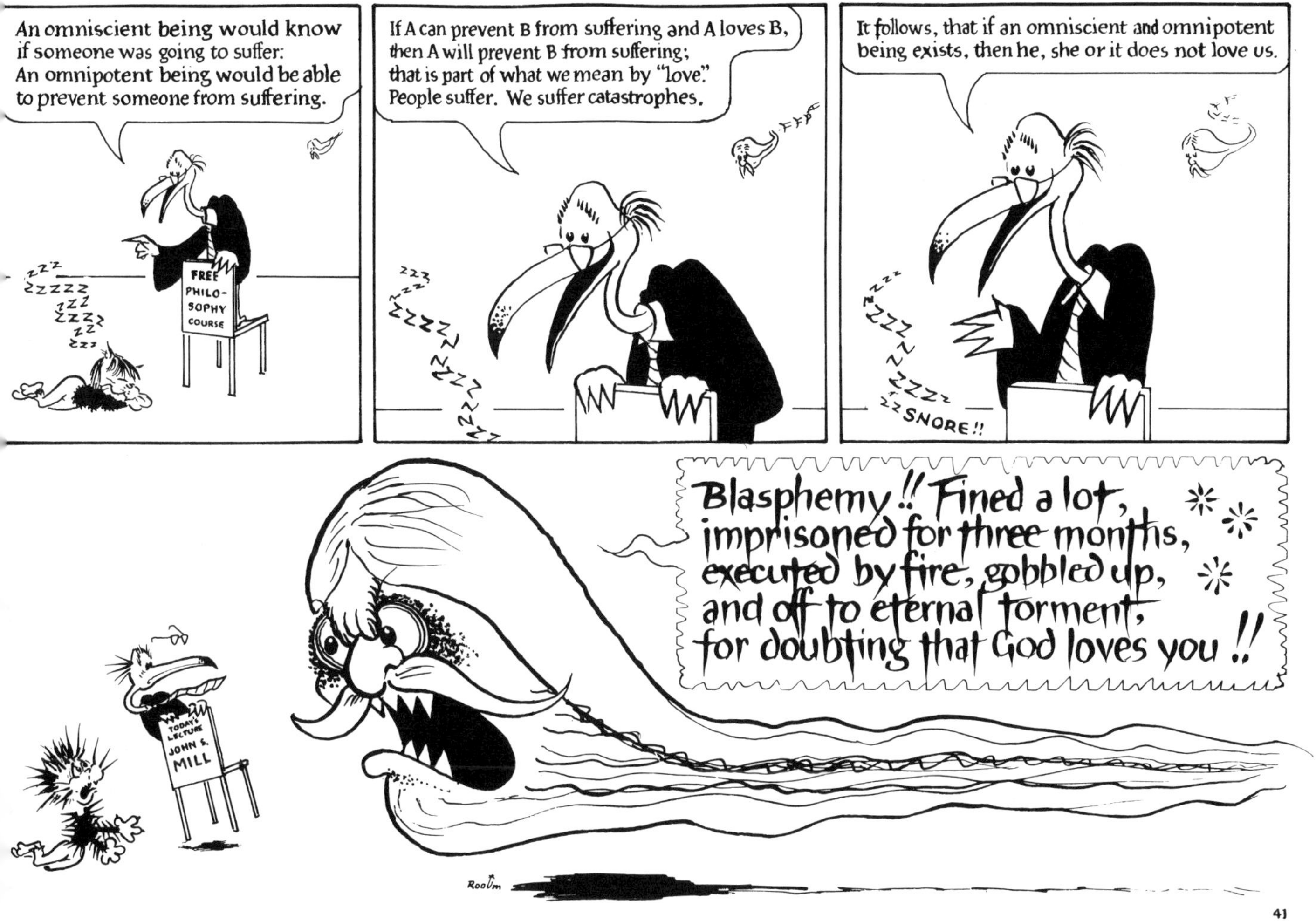
An omniscient being would know if someone was going to suffer: An omnipotent being would be able to prevent someone from suffering.
FREE PHILOSOPHY COURSE
If A can prevent B from suffering and A loves B, then A will prevent B from suffering; that is part of what we mean by "love." People suffer. We suffer catastrophes.
It follows, that if an omniscient and omnipotent being exists, then he, she or it does not love us.
SNORE!!
Blasphemy!! Fined a lot, imprisoned for three months, executed by fire, gobbled up, and off to eternal torment, for doubting that God loves you!!
TODAY'S LECTURE JOHN S. MILL

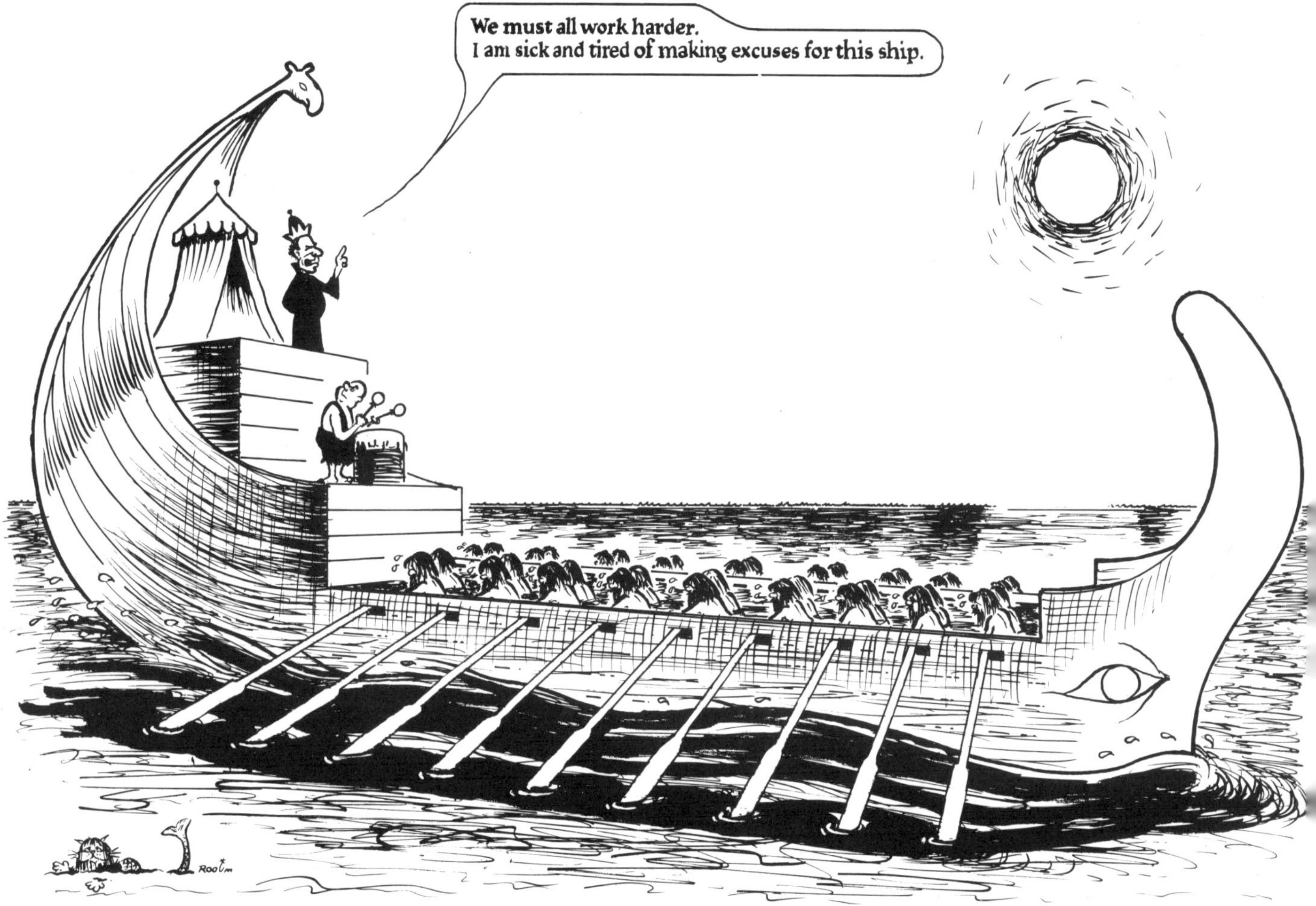
We must all work harder.
I am sick and tired of making excuses for this ship.
Roob'm

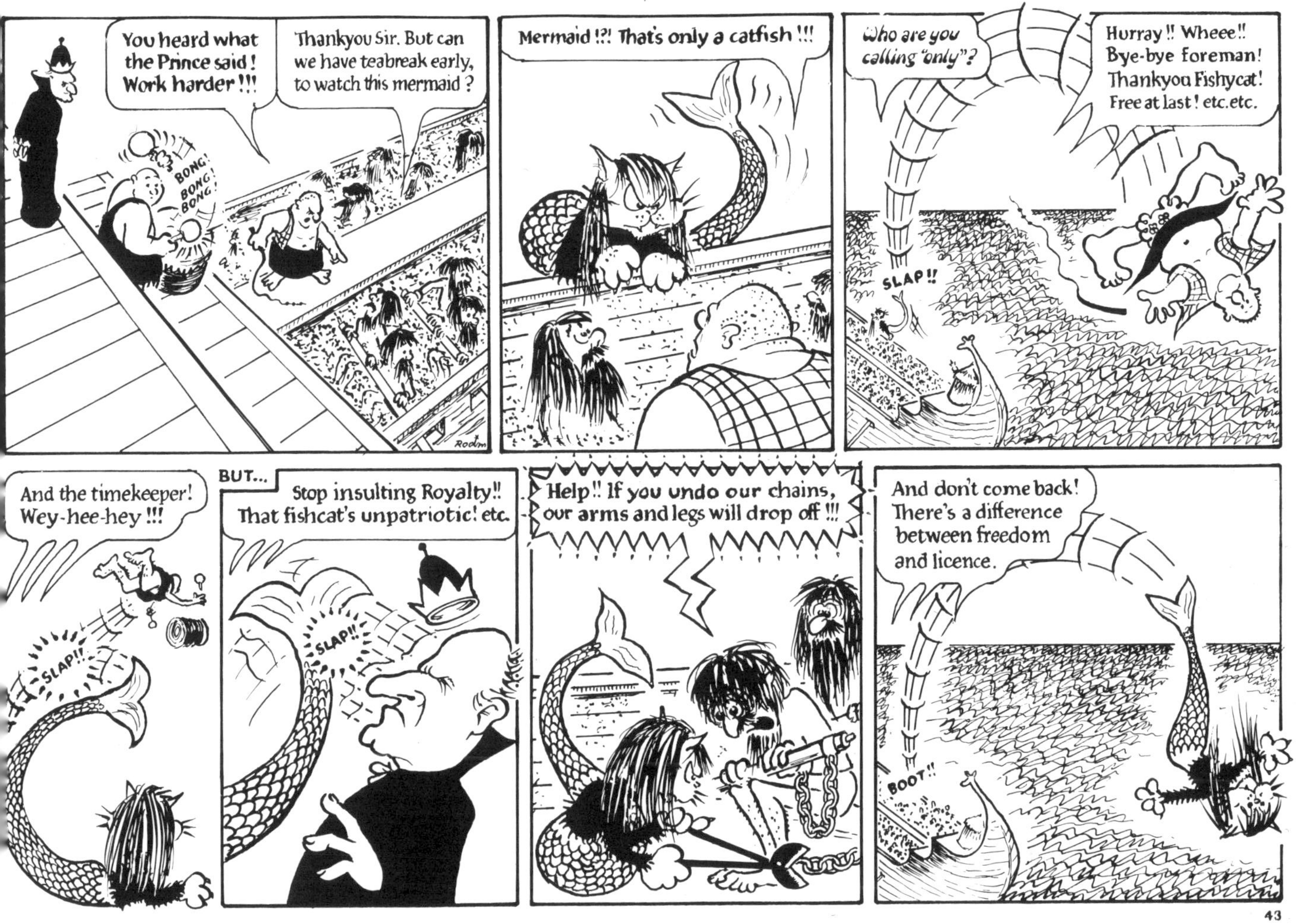
You heard what the Prince said! Work harder!!!
BONG! BONG! BONG!
Thankyou Sir. But can we have teabreak early, to watch this mermaid?
Mermaid !?! That's only a catfish !!!
Who are you calling "only"?
Hurray!! Wheee!! Bye-bye foreman! Thankyou Fishycat! Free at last! etc.etc.
SLAP!!
And the timekeeper! Wey-hee-hey!!!
SLAP!!
BUT...
Stop insulting Royalty!! That fishcat's unpatriotic! etc.
SLAP!!
Help!! If you undo our chains, our arms and legs will drop off!!!
And don't come back! There's a difference between freedom and licence.
BOOT!!

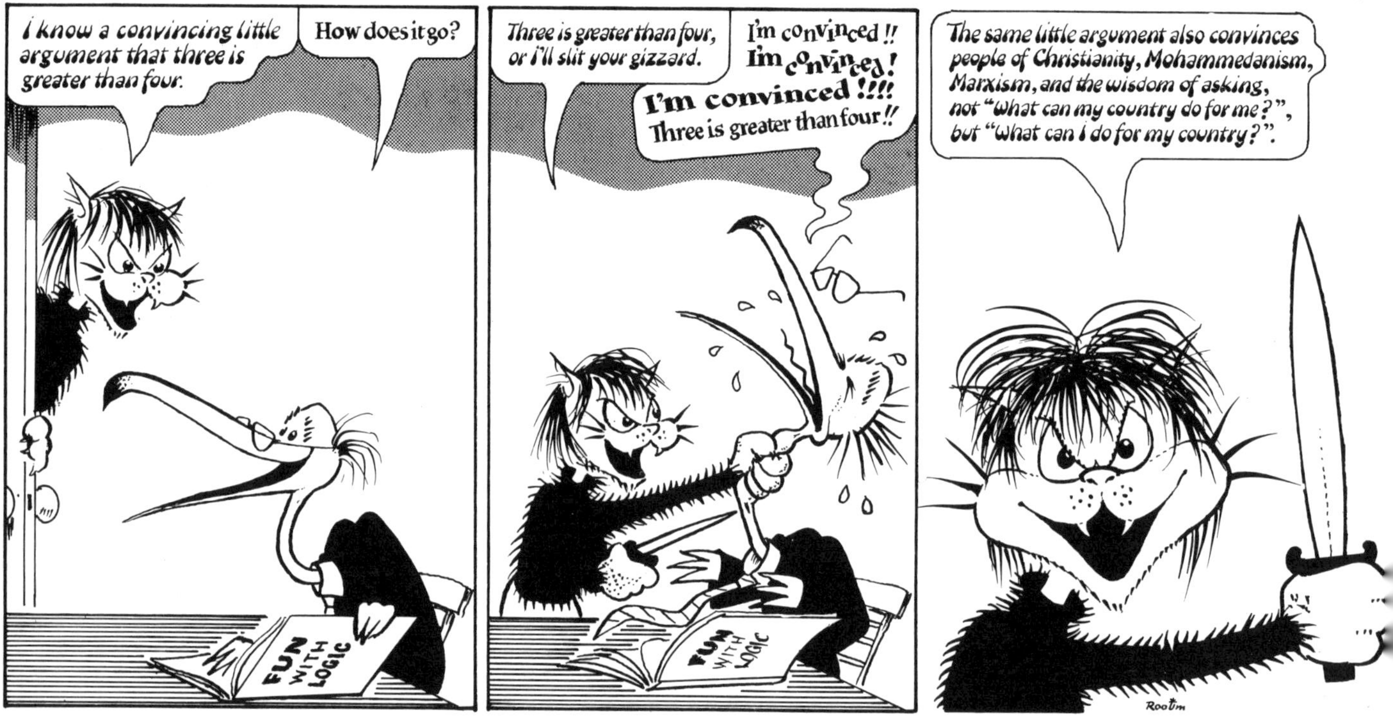
I know a convincing little argument that three is greater than four.
How does it go?
Three is greater than four, or I'll slit your gizzard.
I'm convinced !!
I'm convinced !
I'm convinced !!!!
Three is greater than four !!
The same little argument also convinces people of Christianity, Mohammedanism, Marxism, and the wisdom of asking, not "What can my country do for me?", but "What can I do for my country?".
FUN WITH LOGIC
FUN WITH LOGIC
Rooum

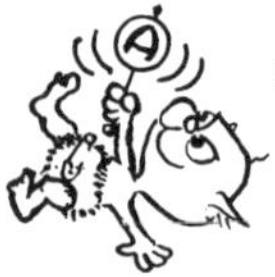

HISTORY NOTE. The drawing opposite was published in *Wildcat* in 1975, when the Pussycat was smaller.
The Parable of the Good Shepherd, on the two pages following, was first published in *Anarchy* in 1964.